"Ashley has shared the truth in a profo
enables readers to enter into her brok
to join in her truth-telling. In a world h.
perfection, this book makes the most bro
                    Bianca Juarez Olt.   ...er, and
                        bestselling .   ...r ot *Play with Fire*

"First of all, I simply love Ashley and believe in her unique voice.
I found myself laughing out loud and shouting amen, all while
being captivated by each story and Scripture, broken down in ways
that brought new perspective. Practical, personal, and powerful,
Rise of the Truth Teller will cause you to dig deep, open your eyes,
and ask some real questions while being compelled to face yourself
honestly, walk in wholeness with Jesus, and rise up."
          Andi Andrew, author, speaker, host of the *Coffee with Andi*
                        podcast, founder of She Is Free, and
                                cofounder of Liberty Church

"*Rise of the Truth Teller* has much insight and wisdom desperately
needed in a time when many women are experiencing an identity
crisis. This must-read reminds us that our lives are not our own
and glorifying God is the ultimate fulfillment of life. Though you
will find yourself challenged by the convictions laid out in this
text, by the end you will undoubtedly be blessed and inspired to
confidently be who God has called you to be!"
          Heather Lindsey, founder of Pinky Promise, author, and speaker

"Through a wise, engaging, and poignant voice, Ashley helps us
realize not only the power of our own story but the freedom that
comes from fully embracing it without shame or regret. She weaves
together tangible steps for each of us to follow to take off our
masks and enter into relationships that can help us heal and thrive.
I highly recommend this book to anyone looking to reengage with
their heart, truly trust again, and live peacefully in the beautiful
tension of the process."
          Sarah Dubbeldam, CEO and editor in chief of Darling Media

"Ashley's authenticity, insightful reflections, lived experience, and
loving truth telling will invite readers to live the bravely honest
and meaningful lives we were designed for. Also, there is no doubt
in my mind that Ashley will be recognized as one of the most
incredible writers of our time. So, even if you aren't ready to take

off the mask or get woke, you will still enjoy her brilliant use of the English language."

Harmony (Dust) Grillo, founder of Treasures and author of *Scars & Stilettos*

"Ashley shares good old-fashioned truths we all need to hear, no matter what season of life we find ourselves in. Like us, Ashley is no stranger to heartache, loss, grief, and struggle, and she reminds us, page after page, that truth and grace are tucked in every corner of our lives, given to us by the Truth himself."

Tiffany Bluhm, author of *She Dreams* and cohost of the *Why Tho* podcast

"Ashley Abercrombie has truly written the book of the hour! It is so relevant and raw. We live in a world of 'fake.' Nothing is as it seems, but this is the season where we must come clean by airing our dirty laundry that has never been placed in the washing machine of God's grace. May we all develop a new level of transparency and vulnerability that will create deeper bonds with one another instead of the bondage that results from pretending we are perfect."

Maria Durso, author and pastor of Christ Tabernacle

"Ashley proves that the truth, the honest truth, is an invitation to the table. When she shares vulnerably about her life, her experiences, her journey—something deep inside of you boldly rises to meet her. *Rise of the Truth Teller* is timely and timeless, funny and sobering, confronting and full of compassion at every turn. It's refreshing to see someone write a book this poignant. I believe with all of my heart that Ashley rising to be a truth-teller will set generations free to do the same."

Courtney Lopez, president of West of Fairfax

"Ashley is not afraid of telling the truth in her new book, *Rise of the Truth Teller*. Get ready to laugh and cry, and be refreshed by her real and raw stories. Her vulnerability and transparency are contagious! I feel more courageous and ready to own my story and rise to be a truth teller!"

Monica Ahn, pastor, speaker, and advocate

"*Rise of the Truth Teller* is powerful, hilarious, deep, transformative, and such a timely word for women of every age and ethnicity! I laughed, I cried, I couldn't put it down, and most of all I felt like hope and freedom were imparted into my soul. I have the privilege of knowing Ashley, and my goodness, that woman is the real deal. Her passion for God and people and her pursuit of kingdom justice are astounding and contagious."

Jennifer Toledo, author, colead pastor of Expression 58 Church, Los Angeles, and founder of The Justice Group

"With deep, personal, and pastoral conviction and writing with gut-level candor and wit, Ashley shares the need to move beyond our masks and completely embrace the honesty of our humanity. The message of her book calls the reader to engage the process of truth telling, affirming the integrity and freedom it brings, further moving people toward much-needed individual and collective restoration."

Michelle Ferrigno Warren, activist and author of
The Power of Proximity

"In *Rise of the Truth Teller*, Ashley Abercrombie feels as if she is across the table holding your hand, sharing her story and championing you through yours. Ultimately, she fearlessly declares God's hope if we are willing to acknowledge and accept who we are and whose we are. This book is a challenge to every faith-filled person to look inside our soul and reveal the truth we may be trying to hide, to 'name it and tame it' and to pursue power, reconciliation, and justice."

Mandy Cook, wife, mom of two, and owner of Chick-fil-A, Fulton Street, Manhattan

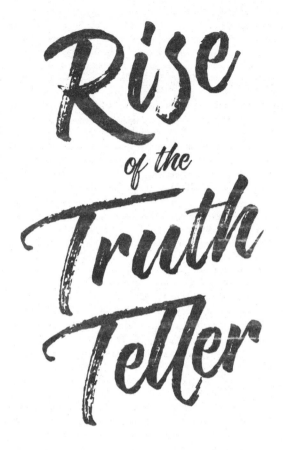

Rise of the Truth Teller

Own Your Story, Tell It Like It Is,
and Live with Holy Gumption

ASHLEY ABERCROMBIE

BakerBooks

a division of Baker Publishing Group
Grand Rapids, Michigan

© 2019 by Ashley Abercrombie

Published by Baker Books
a division of Baker Publishing Group
PO Box 6287, Grand Rapids, MI 49516-6287
www.bakerbooks.com

Printed in the United States of America

Library of Congress Cataloging-in-Publication Data
Names: Abercrombie, Ashley, 1975– author.
Title: Rise of the truth teller : own your story, tell it like it is, and live with holy gumption / Ashley Abercrombie.
Description: Grand Rapids : Baker Books, a division of Baker Publishing Group, 2019. | Includes bibliographical references.
Identifiers: LCCN 2019006886 | ISBN 9780801094385 (pbk. : alk. paper)
Subjects: LCSH: Christian women—Religious life. | Integrity—Religious Aspects—Christianity. | Storytelling—Religious aspects—Christianity. | Witness bearing (Christianity)
Classification: LCC BV4527 .A24 2019 | DDC 248.8/43—dc23
LC record available at https://lccn.loc.gov/2019006886

The author is represented by The Christopher Ferebee Agency, www.christopherferebee.com.

19 20 21 22 23 24 25   7 6 5 4 3 2 1

If you find yourself exhausted from pretending and performing, weary of wearing a mask, you are not alone. It is possible to come out of hiding, break the silence, and live a life that matters. There's plenty of space and grace for you to be your whole self with God and with others. There's something in you the world needs, and we aren't the same without you. I'm glad you're here. Welcome.

To my wonderful husband and life partner, Cody Abercrombie: your love freed me up to be who I thought I could be. It's so good to have a safe corner of the earth where truth is not a threat but a lifeline. I'm in this with you always, even though you insist on singing the Texas state song.

CONTENTS

Part Three LIVE WITH HOLY GUMPTION

Part One

OWN YOUR STORY

one

THE TRUTH ABOUT YOUR PAST

Taking Off the Mask
Because My Story Matters

> There is no greater agony than bearing an untold story inside you.
>
> Maya Angelou, *I Know Why the Caged Bird Sings*

The first time I heard another woman tell her story, I clutched my heart and gasped. Could this be true? Are these things we actually talk about? Abuse, shame, failure, all the messes we make, and the struggles we go through—could there be an honest life on the other side of it all? I remember thinking, *If she's so free to share this, then maybe it's possible for me to be free as well.* She gave me hope that the gap between who I was and who I was pretending to be could finally start closing.

The power of her story helped me take my first steps toward freedom. She taught me a truth that day:

My story matters.

She went first, and that gift of going second is precious to me. The wisdom I've gleaned from walking alongside people who got the thing I wanted, or who walked through hell and back with me at their side—well, sister, you can't put a price on that. I have witnessed courage in the darkest corners of another's life; faith when there was no tangible evidence to back belief; strange beauty found in guttural cries of sorrow, in eyes intense with rage, in hands and hearts choosing to give in the worst of circumstances; and exceeding joy as friends birthed a child, wrote a book, overcame an addiction, or quit something that needed to be quit.

Lord knows I have cheered them on, wept by their side, believed, prayed, and hoped for their dream as if the dream were mine. And I'd be lying if I told you that I hadn't also ached inside with longing, battled jealousy, felt out of place, and wondered when my time would come and if I'd only ever watch others get the thing I want.

Can you believe how hard it is to be human? Have you ever really thought about it? The stress of life, the annoying little things (like my butt shifting farther south the closer I get to forty. What. Is. Happening?), the relational challenges (literally locking myself in a bathroom to keep from losing it with my child, and also a coworker), the financial struggles (Why do I have to pay bills instead of get massages?), the loss, and the grief. Nothing about it is easy. And that's why sharing our lives, our memories, our dreams, and our pain is critical to our sanity and survival.

Our stories matter. Many of us suffer in silence and wonder if we are alone in our pain. The truth about our past has the power to heal. When we are the first to share; the first to be vulnerable; the first to bravely face and overcome abuse, failure, shame, or addiction; or the first to forgive, dream again, or be a true friend, it helps us realize that we are not alone and that we are not crazy. When another person we love and respect normalizes our lived experiences and our confusing emotions, we exhale; we decide we're going to be okay and that we just might make it through this (whatever "this" is). We're encouraged and inspired to respond. And maybe, someday, we'll even be moved to do the same for another—to go first.

I've told many of my stories, sometimes as a response and sometimes as a risk, but it's nearly always been worth it. Except for one time on a Christian television show. I'll tell you about that later, but for now, if you've never had a sister go first, may I go first with you? Because I believe you've got the makings of a truth teller. I believe you've got some stories to tell, some hard-earned wisdom we need.

So, here we go: my story.

I found out I was pregnant the first time in a Texaco gas station bathroom. It was close to midnight in Raleigh, North Carolina, where I had recently attended a local university. I was back visiting for a long weekend, after losing my full-ride academic scholarship. I no longer had an apartment in the city where I had lived for my first two years out of high school. Instead, I had moved home and gotten a job at Sagebrush Steakhouse in Reidsville. One day I noticed my work jeans felt snug at the waist and hips. I went to the restroom, and sure enough, the lower part of my tummy seemed firm and round.

I hadn't thrown up in a while. Now that I was back home, without academic pressure to perform hanging over my head and with a move to Los Angeles on the horizon, I seemed to be getting better. I was taking regular Pilates classes and eating the best I could in a small town to curb my desire to binge and purge, so my jeans fitting tight wasn't because of the usual swelling of an eating disorder.

By the time I made the two-hour drive to Raleigh that weekend, my equilibrium felt off and I was nauseous. So, after spending some time with friends, I went to a gas station and bought a pregnancy test. I felt too afraid to call a friend and too ashamed to take the test in someone's home. I locked the gas station's only bathroom, peed on the stick, and placed it on the back of the toilet.

I crouched down in the corner and started to pray. "Please, God, please. I can't be pregnant. I've gone through so much, and I'm two weeks away from starting over. Please, please, God, don't let me be pregnant."

With my gut in my throat and tears streaming down my face, I took the long walk to the test.

Positive.

I had dreamed my whole life about becoming a mother. Maybe I'd bake something to let my husband know, or get one of those fancy silver something-or-others from Tiffany's, make dinner, and have it wrapped on his place setting. We'd celebrate together in our home and start talking nursery colors and names. It would be one of the happiest moments of my life.

This was among the most painful.

I was born in Eden, North Carolina, at the only hospital in town. It was a beautiful beginning place, small enough to know everybody and to rarely know anyone at all. We all had secrets, because that is what humans keep, and as sweet as my childhood was, perhaps the skill I retained best was masking my pain.

I don't fully understand why I felt compelled to hide, to retreat deep inside myself, to swallow every hurt and wound and keep myself from burdening others, but I did. I don't have anyone to blame; still, we all make choices based on our context, on what has shaped and informed us, and until we know different, we do the best we can with what we have.

I don't know if it's like this everywhere, but in the South we are raised to tell the truth. And most of the time, that means telling it like it is . . . about other people. "That girl is homely." "Honey, he is mean as a rattlesnake." "I told her he's a low-down, dirty scoundrel, and he's dumb as a brick too, but she don't listen." "Well, you know she ain't the sharpest tool in the shed." "That teacher is busier than a one-armed wallpaper hanger. She makes me a nervous wreck."

There's a small exchange, and it often starts with, "Well, you know . . . " and ends with, "Bless her heart." Which is no kind of blessing, let me tell you. Hand over heart, I have howled at these hilarious sayings while secretly creating characters for a future novel. But growing up, I had no understanding of the power of words. They shape our worldview, tearing people down or building them up, dictating the tone of our lives and relationships. Words both explicit and implicit, particularly when we are young and especially from those in close proximity whom we love and admire, teach us our own value as well as what we should value.

For example, if the direct and indirect judgment we hear is often about the way a woman looks, we might take away that skinny women with little thighs, blonde hair, and tan skin are the only beautiful kind of women, and spend a lifetime looking down on others or trying to live up to an impossible standard ourselves.

This kind of truth is the dangerous kind, because it's rooted in judgment and approval. Its giver decides what's pretty, who's smart, what's best. Usually, he or she assumes little to no personal responsibility and fosters an environment that demands others absorb all the fault and accusation, change and fix themselves to fit in, and potentially take care of everyone and make things right for everybody. It's not truth; it's pretending. Pretending to be sweet. Pretending not to be controlling. Pretending to be perfect. All hail the know-it-all, or the silent manipulator, or the dominant abuser who decides what's best for everyone else, including their worth, capability, and future.

I grew up smack-dab in the middle of this doctrine, and all I know is I learned how to hide all the ugly. I also learned to tell everybody else what they should and shouldn't do. I can't even say I did that well; I didn't even know what I should be doing half the time, much less what anybody else should do. In my wake were the people affected by my inability to live with integrity, to be forthcoming about my own life and story in response to another's honesty. When I loved, I loved well. And when I didn't, well, I didn't. I don't recall being nasty to others, but I had a habit of saying goodbye whenever someone got close to my truth without any input from the person on the other side. #Byefelicia. Sometimes I ran because the relationship was dangerous in the first place, and when I realized it I pulled out quickly. And sometimes a friendship was salvageable but I didn't know how to tell the truth about how the relationship was affecting me. I didn't understand reciprocity, only giving and saving or the shame that comes from owing.

Real truth telling requires intimacy and vulnerability. Knowing when to walk away and when to stay, what to share and when and how to share it, requires maturity. Becoming a healthy friend in healthy relationship is a ton of work. Getting honest is no picnic. Our deepest wounds come from relationships with others. Unfortunately, our growth and healing depend on our willingness to peel back the layers of comfort and security we hide behind, in order to reengage, trust again, and try again with others.

This requires us to take off our mask and risk showing all the ugly to discover that we are worthy of love despite our past, our flaws, and our fear. This requires us to get honest about who we are, where we are, who we want to be, and where we want to go, inviting others to live inside that gap with us and committing to stand in theirs as well. Truth telling takes guts and gumption, grit and grace. And our world has never needed us to buck up, buttercup, more than it does right now.

This is the rise of the truth teller.

I was eighteen when I left my hometown for college, and I was already a few degrees off the path I'd decided to pursue. Toward the end of my senior year, I started drinking and smoking weed. Weary from people pleasing and trying to live up to both my own standard of perfection and the standard I perceived from everyone else, I started to buckle under the pressure. I had secured an academic scholarship and would be leaving home for the first time. Eden, the town where I was

19

raised, had just over fourteen thousand people. The college I was attending had twenty-eight thousand students. Academia was a strong suit, but I was used to small classrooms, where teachers knew my name and often spent time encouraging me and helping me rise to my potential.

When I showed up for my first chemistry class and there were three hundred people sitting in stadium-style seating, I freaked out. I smiled, made my way to the top row, and figured I was going to fail. I was right, by the way; I sure did fail chemistry. (Twice. Bless.) And even my replacement grade the next semester was a low C. I didn't know how to flourish in that environment. Friends were pledging sororities and parties were easy to find, along with alcohol and free weed, if wanted.

At the same time, my parents separated after twenty-four years of marriage, which really was the best choice they could have made. Still, I was away at school and my younger brother was at home. Things happened so fast that our house was sold by the time I made it back for a visit. In less than a year, all the stability in my life had transitioned into an unknown future, and I didn't know what to do. I had a few close friends on campus, but I still withheld how I was feeling, sharing information only and not allowing myself to be vulnerable or scared. I thought everyone expected me to be the strong one, so that's the role I played, which is unfortunate because it made me a terrible friend. I'm sure people thought that nothing was ever wrong with me, and honestly, who wants to be friends with a person like that? It was unfair and one-sided, but at the time it was the only kind of friendship I knew how to have.

My inability to take off my mask and engage in reciprocal friendship cost me. My existence, outside of people pleasing and performing, felt like a burden to others. The thought of sharing a hard truth about myself scared me into silence. I felt ashamed of my struggles and I hated feeling like a burden. Without the capacity to share my pain, I began to self-harm to relieve the internal pressure I experienced from not having many healthy outlets to tell the truth. I lived in constant fear that if people really knew me, if they knew how much I needed them to help me, then they would leave me or reject me.

To cope, I developed an eating disorder. Bulimia. I remember the first time I made the decision to throw up; I was in the shower in my dorm. I grabbed my belly, full of disdain and disgust. To tell you the truth, I don't even know where I learned to do this. I didn't read about it; I didn't watch anyone else; it's as if I had known how to do this all my life. Like I had been led right here, subtly and slowly, over a lifetime, to this moment, when I turned all the things I could not control into rage against myself. Bulimia continued the cycle of shame and, in turn, left me needing something more effective at numbing the pain. My coping arsenal grew to include smoking weed and drinking like a fish. It wasn't long before it expanded into ecstasy pills and partying nearly every night with friends. While I enjoyed the feeling of significance being the life of the party gave me, depression, anxiety, and heartache were the unwelcome companions joining me as I cried myself to sleep many nights. I had a King James Version of the Bible, from my childhood, that I put under my pillow. The words didn't make sense to me at all (Hello, I don't read or speak Shakespeare), so I rarely read it, but I prayed somehow that God would get something good inside my head so I could quit hurting myself. Meanwhile, I was taking a full load of classes, keeping my GPA up for my scholarship, working part-time, and participating as an athlete on the crew team.

At the end of that first year, I took a job as a resident assistant in my dorm, which provided free housing through the summer. I continued to avoid authentic relationships by setting myself up as a person others came to for advice or to share their problems. By the time they asked me how I was, I could offer only a general response. People felt close to me, and often would call me one of their closest friends—but I didn't actually know how to be close. I knew how to meet needs but couldn't share my own. I knew how to encourage dreams but kept mine hidden. I knew how to give to others but had no idea how to receive from them. There's nothing quite like feeling incredibly lonely even though you're constantly surrounded by people.

My hometown had successfully raised me to share everything and absolutely nothing at all.

Things came to a head right before my second year of college. Our dorm hosted kids for athletic camps during the summer. The coaches were students from other universities who stayed all summer. In that mix was a guy I didn't know well, other than saying hello in the lobby and seeing him out at night, sometimes dancing with our crew. There was a nightclub next to campus that, unfortunately, turned a blind eye to underage drinking.

Let me pause here and say this: violence against women and sexual exploitation do not happen in isolation; they are endorsed and encouraged with community support. A nightclub that regularly hosts vulnerable, underage, drunk girls; a college dorm full of adults who watch young women coming home wasted, night after night, without taking action; a neighbor who sees something but refuses to get involved in "other people's business"; a family member who suspects a violation but chooses denial, or who hears a victim share but ignores or minimizes their story—these are all complicit.

With the cycle of destruction I was caught up in, it was only a matter of time before something tragic happened. On opening weekend of my sophomore year of college, I was once again drunk and partying in my room with "friends." I vaguely remember a crowd of people, then there were just a few of us— and the next thing I remember is opening my eyes and seeing my underwear on the floor. That image is still so vivid; it's what I stared at until he was finished. I had been raped by the guy from the lobby I barely knew, in my own dorm room. For the longest time, I thought I deserved it. We had danced together once or twice at the club. Maybe I'd asked for it. I blamed myself. *If I hadn't been drinking, this never would have happened.*

But I have come to realize that a person who willfully preys on the vulnerable always, *always* makes the victim feel at fault for their crime. **In the case of sexual assault, they don't just want to take a body; they want to take a voice.**

One in every five women is sexually assaulted while in college in America. Rape is the most underreported crime in our country, and more than 90 percent of sexual assault victims on college campuses do not report the crime.* I remember when a young woman came forward in our dorm about her sexual assault. Within six months, she transferred completely out of our school because rumors had spread that she was a slut and had made a sex tape. A woman's reputation is nearly always tarnished when she comes forward, which is why so many of us

---

*"Statistics about Sexual Violence," National Sexual Violence Resource Center, accessed February 20, 2019, http://www.nsvrc.org/sites/default/files/publications _nsvrc_factsheet_media-packet_statistics-about-sexual-violence_0.pdf.

do not. It doesn't feel worth it to tell our story, to suffer more emotional duress only to have our predator walk away as if nothing had happened.

The next morning I traded my early shift with a coworker and then went back to sleep, and when I woke up later that afternoon I went to work as if nothing had happened. I wouldn't talk about that night for another two and a half years. I chilled out on drugs and drank less, but my struggle with bulimia increased. My motivation began to dwindle. I slept all the time, and skipping class and losing focus became the norm. I retreated from my friends, blaming my busy schedule of school, work, and crew practice. I was living through my days, but mentally I was not present. For the life of me, I cannot even remember a single teacher's name from my college years. I remember moments and conversations, but I do not recall their names. And not even once did a professor ask how I was doing or check in on me, other than the dean of my program once—to remind me to pull my grades up or lose my scholarship. They had high expectations for a student with a full ride, and I better not waste it. Of course, he was right to do so, though I wish he'd done more to try to understand why my grades were slipping. I am also confident that if he had taken the time to try to see what was happening right in from of him, I probably would have lied, smiled, and told him I'd work harder and do better.

When I decided I needed help, the only thing I could afford was a counselor on campus. Lucky for me, her sister had struggled with an eating disorder and she specialized in that field. We were able to talk through my triggers, and a few minor things as well, but I couldn't bring myself to tell her what had happened to me; specifically, the rape. After several sessions, she was at a loss for what to do and suggested I see a psychiatrist.

He spent about thirty minutes with me, and without hearing my story diagnosed me with post-traumatic stress disorder as well as borderline personality disorder, then swiftly prescribed Prozac and another anti-depressant that I've since forgotten, and told me to come back and see him in a month.

I thought he was out of his mind, using all kinds of big, fancy doctor words to scare me and take my money, so I never went back to either therapist again. My skepticism served me well in this case, because I needed safe space to get honest and friendships to help me grow rather than prescription drugs. For the record, I do believe in modern medicine, and sometimes we do need a prescription to help us stabilize, to heal us, alongside our recovery.

The psychiatrist was wrong about the personality disorder, but he was right about the PTSD. A dark hole of shame was swallowing me up. I didn't understand why I couldn't recover and move on. I thought something was seriously wrong with me, and because I assumed the rape was my fault, the shame was compounded. It pressed me further into hiding, and the only way I knew how to break the silence was to binge and purge. It felt like the only emotional release in my life.

Before the end of that school year, I started dating a friend. He didn't like drugs and alcohol, so I quit them, except on special occasions. My grades remained subpar, and I decided double workouts and hitting the water by 5:30 a.m. were too much for my mental state, so I quit crew. I worked more hours at my waitressing job, made good money, and felt I was doing all right for myself. After making it through the summer incident-free, I thought my life was moving in the right direction. Mentally and emotionally, I was growing stronger, but at the start of my junior year, I just couldn't hack it academically. In danger of losing my scholarship, I figured the best thing to do was give it up.

Sitting in the office of the dean of admissions, I wanted so badly to tell him that I wasn't a failure, that there were other circumstances hindering me from achieving my goal of finishing school. Inside I was pleading for help, but I couldn't form the words with my lips. My legs felt like cement as I walked away from his office. You know that slow motion effect that happens in movies, where the crowd around the character blurs and there's no real sound except for an empty ringing? That's what happened to me. I stayed in my dorm the rest of the afternoon, not talking, not doing, just lying on my bed, staring at my ceiling. I felt gutted, numb, and overwhelmed by the thought of telling my mom, my friends, and my family that I had failed.

Sometimes, to relieve stress, I would buy a pack of menthols and just drive. But later that night, I bought a coffee and drove to an empty parking lot. The sky opened up, sharing my sorrow, dumping sheets of rain. I wrote furiously in my journal as I sat there, sobbing. Then I started to scream at God, "Where are you? WHERE ARE YOU!?" When I had emptied myself of fury, I allowed myself to admit what I had not yet had the courage to say: "My life is completely out of control. I need help."

Just saying it out loud broke the hold silence had on me. It felt like a river ran through me, cleansing me, warming the cold parts of me. Giving myself space to be out of control and honest, for once, about my need gave me a taste of freedom. I wanted more. In this moment, the mask came off for the first time as I expressed my emotions without any brokering and allowed myself to be right where I was without measuring against the past or bowing to the impossible expectation to be perfect. In the days and weeks to come, I started to try to dream again, to consider what might be possible beyond the pit of my problems.

My experience with faith began in a small Southern Baptist church, a gathering of down-home good people that had potlucks and a library in the basement by the fellowship hall. My great-great-aunt Fairy started taking me to church when I was just a baby. In 1988, as a seven-year-old, I walked down the aisle during the old hymn "I Surrender All" and told our pastor, Mr. Freeman, that I wanted to follow Jesus. Then I stood and shook all seventy hands of the congregants, who welcomed me into the Christian faith. In a white dress, I was baptized in front of my family and faith community. In the children's ministry, my teachers taught me Bible stories, showed me how to pray for missionaries, and helped me experience the love of Jesus. I served with Aunt Fairy, picking and arranging flowers for the altar from her massive garden, opening the church doors, and watching her help people choose books from the library. However, at sixteen I left the church, unsure of my place as one of the only teenagers there, and I struggled to connect my questions, fears, and insecurities to my faith in Christ. I didn't go back until I was twenty-one.

That moment in the parking lot not only broke the shame of silence but opened my heart again to God. He is never afraid of our circumstances. He doesn't leave us alone in our mistakes and failures. He doesn't avoid us until we get our act together. He is present in our pain. He loves us, always, no matter what we do. Accepting myself as I was began to reset my trajectory.

My heart craved a new beginning. I made the decision to continue my studies in Los Angeles, hoping to start over, to leave it all behind without any connection to my past. I left school and my jobs as a resident assistant and a waitress, moved home, and started working at that steakhouse in Reidsville with a plan in place to move three thousand miles away.

After discovering my pregnancy that night at the Texaco station, I sat in my car, stunned. The weight of reality and the pain of what felt like another failure overwhelmed me, and while I don't remember much about my mental state, I know I did not allow myself to feel much of anything. My coping mechanisms were hiding and fixing, so I got to fixing as quickly as possible.

I called an abortion clinic and made an appointment for the next day, sometime in January. The details are still fuzzy. With a gun to my head, I couldn't tell you today where the office was, but I know the appointment was sometime in the midmorning. I distinctly remember the rectangle shape of the room we were herded into, office chairs lining three walls with a dozen other women forced to face each other. An old, thick television hung on the wall, dusty and grey. Objects remain in my memory but not faces, and this is the burden of trauma, of disassociation: the need to focus on details that matter less and deny, bury, or endure those that matter most. I can't remember if the aide was tall or short, if her skin was light or dark, if she had a soft voice or not, if she was kind or clinical. But she turned on an informational video to tell us how we'd feel before, during, and after abortion. I honed in on the small cup she'd given each of us. It had a blue pill in it—Valium. My stomach turned; I left the room, distraught.

A life, a baby boy or girl, was inside me. How could I go through with this? My hands were shaking, my chest tightened; I was absolutely devastated. The same aide found me and led me into one of the offices, where I sat for a few minutes, feeling faint. The light from the windows in the office blurred her face in my memory, but I do recall her asking me how I was doing and offering me another Valium. After a few more minutes alone, I needed help to walk to the next room, where I decided to go through with the abortion. I can only recall my time in the actual procedure in snapshots: my knees, my chest, my feet in stirrups, a hand, the doctor's glasses, a shadow on each side of me assisting the doctor.

In the recovery room, I sat in one of what looked like a row of dental chairs with the same women I had watched the video with. It looked more like a Red Cross center than an abortion clinic. But I had not given life. I had taken it.

On the way home, the combination of muscle relaxers and laughing gas and anguish made me hysterical. Laughter left my lips but tears poured down my face, and this only added to my sorrow and shame. That evening, when I could speak again, I told the father of my baby, "I never want to speak about this again. Do you understand me? I never want to say another word about this." I rolled over into a fetal position, curled a blanket around me, and prayed I would never wake up.

I turned twenty-one that February of 2002, and not even two weeks later drove across the country to Los Angeles to start a new life.

My mom was with me, and we decided to drive straight to the ocean. Listening to the waves crashing helped me breathe. I closed my eyes to inhale the salty air, feeling its moisture on my skin. Then, exhaling, I stood staring at the beauty of the West Coast. With a knowing in my gut, I whispered, "I'm home." Mom cried because she knew it too, and I felt peace wash over me. There, by the waters of the Pacific Ocean, I felt as though the expectations of others had lifted from me. The failure I had become, the mistakes I had made, could be forgotten. I could leave it all behind.

But I'd soon learn: **everywhere you go, there you are.**

A long road to recovery was ahead of me, but so were rich relationships, marriage and babies, inspiring faith, opportunities to use my voice and make a difference, and the determination to discover what I was born to do and do it.

The world is hungry for people to own their stories and to create safe spaces for others to do the same. We need a release from shame, freedom from fear, and courage to say what needs to be said and do what needs to be done.

It's taken me fifteen years to become a person I love. The pain of continuing has made me want to quit more times than I can count. I've wanted to run fast toward my internal cave of pain while my face smiled and lied and hid. It's been painful to live honestly, to tell the truth and learn to do so with grace and love and without being derogatory, condescending, or judgmental. I still fail at this often, but now I am aware of myself, I can say sorry, and I can walk away from circumstances and people that make me play the game.

Truth telling starts with me.

I don't want to spend another moment pretending and performing. I don't know about you, but I've spent so many years getting rid of my mask that I can't bear to ever wear it again. I'm too old and too annoyed. *Ain't nobody got time for that.* Besides, I've got a raging, colorful past, and now that I can admit it, who am I to judge?

I've stepped out of hiding and it's scary out here, but I've discovered I'm not alone; there's a generous portion of good, imperfect people living on the edge, truth telling with confidence and unabashedly loving themselves, God, and others. Living vulnerably, without all my weapons and walls, defense mechanisms and superwoman tendencies, has made me easier to know. Alongside other powerful women and men who are chasing love and truth relentlessly, I'm still shedding some of the skin I'm in, but I've learned not to mind the process of becoming.

Friend, hang in there. Your story matters, and whatever chapter you're living, remember that you are not alone. You have sisters and brothers in your corner, all over the world, who are fighting the good fight and overcoming impossible odds. You're not finished. This is not the end of the story, so keep on keeping on. You are loved. There's nobody else who can do what you were created to do—you are unique, one of a kind—and God is with you and for you. And please know I'm in this with you. Thank you for taking a chance on me. It's no small thing to give me your time, and I promise to give my best to serve you, to love you, and to journey with you as you process your life and your faith.

My prayer for our time together is that you would laugh out loud and know that you are not alone in your crazy (because we're all a bit north of crazy, given the right conditions, anyway). That you would own your story. That you would create a safe space for others to do the same. That you would rise from the ashes of your past and take hold of the glorious future you are promised. That you would rise as a truth teller, a difference maker, and boldly, without apology, release others to do the same.

RISE, *Truth* TELLER

- Your story matters.
- Violence against women and sexual exploitation do not happen in isolation; they are endorsed and encouraged with community support.
- In the case of sexual assault, they don't just want to take a body; they want to take a voice.
- Truth telling starts with you.

TELL THE *Truth*

- When's the last time a story impacted your life?
- What do you think of the phrase "My story matters"? Did anything in my story resonate with you?
- Hiding and pretending in a relationship makes things complicated. What's been your experience with that in the relationships you've been involved in? How has it affected you?
- What is the importance of a truth teller in our world? Do you know any truth tellers? How have they impacted your life?
- How does your story, and the concept of truth telling, intersect with your faith?

two

THE TRUTH ABOUT FORGIVENESS

My Other Favorite F-Word

> She's got a mouth like a sailor.
>
> All the moms at the Y

I started cussing in the fifth grade, and some of that can be traced directly to my father and some to my craziest uncles, who sat on the porch at my great-grandmother Lucy's house, shooting feral cats and, in general, being a nuisance to God and everybody. The rest of it can be chalked up to the older kids at the YMCA and, of course, free will.

One of my teachers, Mrs. Lester, had a strong penchant for proper English language, and slang from the neighborhood Y was unacceptable in her classroom. I got frustrated once about who knows what, and I shouted, "FFFFF . . . ART." (I think we all know what the initial word was meant to be.) Mrs. Lester slowly walked over to my desk, her long black skirt gliding across the floor, with her white button-up shirt, her hair twisted on top of her head, her black glasses, and her pursed lips all making the moment more dreadful, and asked me if I knew the definition of the word *flatulence*.

"No, ma'am."

"Today, in after-school detention, you can discover what it means."

Great, just what I wanted, to skip an afternoon with my friends at the Y and hang out with Mrs. Lester. When the last bell of the day rang, I made my way to her classroom, and she dropped a Webster's dictionary in front of me with a thud. She pointed to the blackboard and said, "Fill that board with the word and definition." So I began to write: "flatulence, noun, the accumulation of gas in the alimentary canal" about one hundred times. And I made sure to mind my manners in Mrs. Lester's presence.

I still cussed on the yard at the Y, because, *duh*. But those were some brutal consequences for a kid in an academically gifted class. (Okay, a beating would have been brutal, but listen, it was embarrassing. I still had buckteeth and wild, unruly red hair. As a giant who had to wear boy jeans so they would be long enough, I really didn't need Mrs. Lester ruining my life.)

In order to survive and in order to win, I had to act a certain way in specific environments. That was the narrative forming in my young mind. *Adjust yourself accordingly. Become what is required. Do what people desire.* Don't cuss at school unless you're trying to impress friends in a place where the adults can't hear. Do cuss at the Y to fit in with the other kids. Don't "get above your raising" by seeming too educated or smart. Be an easy audience; smile and look pretty. Don't speak unless spoken to, especially around important people. Fight to be heard, and remember: if there is a problem, fix it or control it, and if you can't do one of those, then take it out on yourself. And by no means should you just relax and be yourself—unless you are completely alone and no one is present or watching.

In other words, hide.

I created different personas to please people and to protect myself. Sometimes I was wild, outspoken, and fearless. This confident Ashley appeared when I felt safe and loved—times when I didn't feel the need to perform or pretend. Whenever I got to be wholly myself, whether at the Y, in a classroom, at home, or with friends, I found myself laughing loud, speaking my mind, and doing what was in my heart to do. In another setting, I might be quiet, agreeable, and pleasant. This docile Ashley surfaced when I felt a little out of place, like my whole self would not be welcome at the table. Environments outside of my economic, academic, or athletic bracket made me more earnest to please people in order to be accepted. Other times, I acted indifferent, even though all my alarm bells were ringing inside. This uninterested Ashley emerged whenever I felt unsafe and insecure. When people made fun of me, ignored me, or pushed past my boundaries, I pretended like I didn't care to protect myself, and endured until I could flee the situation.

My life felt disjointed, like puzzle pieces in a box, never fully assembled. Due to my chameleon abilities, I was often out of touch with my body and what I thought, felt, and needed. I didn't always recognize when I was hurting, and if I did, I would work hard to ignore the pain, or even harm myself so I could carry on with the façades. Biting my nails and cuticles down to the quick, medicating with sugar, eating too much, obsessing over a boyfriend, or becoming the teacher's pet were a few of my coping behaviors. As I got older, I used alcohol and drugs, as I shared earlier, and stayed in dysfunctional relationships where I would repeat the trauma. By making myself into what the other person wanted, filling their needs so I could be a perfect savior and they, the perfect mess, I never had to focus on my own mess, needs, dreams, and desires.

When I did have a moment alone, it felt like all my Ashleys got together, trying so hard to just *be* but finding it hard to do more than pity themselves, make up a fantasy future together, beat themselves up for not being perfect, or relive the past by thinking through different scenarios and conversations and what we should have done then. (Anyone else queen of the shower rebuttal, five hours too late? "Well, you know what, Karen, you can just . . .")

I was worn out. With my mind in a sprint, my heart full of anxiety, my muscles knotty and exhausted, I was driving myself up the wall like a confused shapeshifter.

My inability to deal with anything, face my fears, or sit with the truth meant I was living a hidden or masked existence. This kind of existence is no way to live, and it's about as far from being whole as possible. And since I wasn't whole, that meant I wasn't capable of walking in *forgiveness*, my other favorite F-word. Want to know why it's my fave?

Because forgiveness leads to wholeness.

Unless we are healthy and whole, how can we ever rise as truth tellers? How can we ever overcome our past and take hold of our future? We can't, because we'll only be able to see ourselves, others, and the world through the lens of our pain and brokenness. Our habits are formed and our pursuits are decided according to our perspective, so what we see matters and literally determines the trajectory of our life. Without forgiveness, we'll have a chip on our shoulder, a hidden agenda of proving ourselves, winning, or getting back at the people who hurt us. We'll repeat destructive behaviors in our life if we don't surrender, let go, forgive, and move on. When we don't forgive, someone else is controlling our life, even if they've been out of our life for years.

I feel like I should be really good at forgiveness by now. I mean, I have to forgive Anthropologie for never carrying size 11 shoes. (Fine, I can't afford them anyway, but this is about principle and unnecessary discrimination against women over six feet tall.) I forgive myself all the time for rarely answering phone calls (this is not what my phone is for; just text me, this is the digital age). I forgive all the airlines for my knees always touching the seat in front of me and for never being able to stand in the airplane bathroom. And I forgive my toddler all the time for throwing toys at my head, which I subsequently throw away and then have to deal with three-year-old sorrow. I also forgive Target for making me spend $120 instead of just $40 on the diapers, toothpaste, and mascara that I actually came to buy. And, sister, you just read my story—I've had a heck of a lot of real things to forgive.

But I am not always good at forgiveness, especially close to home, which is embarrassing to admit because those I love the most should have my best. Forgiveness should come most naturally to and for my people, right? Because if you know me, then why would you hurt me? (Incidentally, this terrible logic shouldn't allow me to hurt others either, so it's a double whammy, because being perfect in relationship becomes a bigger goal for me than being honest in relationship.) To tell the truth, I'm better with strangers, especially strangers with needs.

At my former church, we had a beautiful food pantry ministry where, on Sundays, families could receive groceries for the week. One Sunday, between services, I was downstairs receiving intake forms and had the opportunity to help and connect with a first-timer from the neighborhood. I packed up her groceries and then we both headed upstairs, me to the bathroom and her to I don't know where. Now, I've been in ministry a long time, and sometimes, well, I hide in the bathroom stall if there is no line and scroll Instagram while I pee. Then I put my phone on the toilet paper stand so I can pull my pants back up. That day, as I was exiting from my stall to attend our third service, my new friend was standing there, waiting to go next.

We had a friendly exchange; I washed my hands and left. I walked to our lobby and realized I didn't have my phone. (Did I mention it was brand new? Not even a week old.) I headed back to the bathroom, where she was now washing her hands, let her know I'd left my phone in the stall, and reached in to grab it. Gone. *There must be some explanation*, I thought. *Maybe I dropped it outside.* I left and checked. Nope. So I asked her, "Do you have my phone? Because I left it in that stall."

"No, I didn't see a phone in there," she said.

"Are you sure? I am 100 percent positive I left it there, and then you went in, and now the phone is missing."

"I definitely don't have your phone," she lied, again.

What was I supposed to do? Snatch her purse? Call security and make a scene? Light her up like a Christmas tree and also be one of her pastors? I don't know, maybe it's the "if someone wants to take your shirt, give them your coat also" verse in the Bible that got me, but I just decided to forgive her. It felt easy, because if you have to steal at church, from the lady who just gave you some groceries, what kind of desperate life are you dealing with? Plus, Jesus said so.

I can't even remember her name now, and I never saw her again, and maybe part of me felt self-righteous and proud to just let it go like that. What's so strange about my human experience is that I can feel those exact same things when I hold on to unforgiveness against someone close to me, or against someone who should know better—you know, like church people. Because Jesus also turned tables over and called people fake (because, legit—they should know better), and a brood of vipers, and whitewashed tombs, I feel justified in not forgiving them because they should know better. *How could they have done this to me? How could they hurt me, or betray me, or abandon me this way?*

Anne Lamott said, "You can safely assume you've created God in your own image when it turns out that God hates all the same people you do."* Ouch, Anne. In both forgiveness and unforgiveness, I sometimes find a way to be right and to confidently declare that God is on my side. And all the while I'm making myself superior in my own eyes at the expense of others, which is pride.

―――――――

When we really think about it, isn't hatred at the heart of unforgiveness? I know it's difficult to look at it this way, because

*Anne Lamott, *Bird by Bird: Some Instructions on Writing and Life* (New York: Anchor Books, 1995), 22.

it's so harsh and so hard to see that we're capable of hating, but we are. If I hunker down and look myself in the eye, I begin to realize that not forgiving and hating others has led me to make some serious vows.

I hate you for raping me, *and I will never be vulnerable when intimate again.*

I hate you for verbally abusing me, *and I will hate myself, my thighs, and my voice from now on.*

I hate you for hoarding all the opportunities at work, *so I will strive and overwork to prove myself to our boss, hoping he will give me opportunities too.*

I hate that you never listen to me, *so I will fight to be heard, no matter how contentiously.*

I hate that you hurt me, *so I will suffer in silence and remove my contribution from this project, this team, this church, because you don't see my value and it's not (you're not) worth the fight.*

I hate how blind you are to the issues in our world, and I am so tired of explaining and trying to help you get it, *so I will quit trying to journey in understanding with you.*

This particular people group has always been unkind to me, *so I will judge them and avoid them and hate them in my heart.*

Besides pride, vows are the biggest problem I see with unforgiveness. The power of making these promises in my heart was—and is—that it shatters my true sense of self and sabotages my future. Vows rooted in hatred become a curse. Our vows, spoken and unspoken, can cause us to forfeit our freedom, and that includes the potential fulfillment of a dream, friendships and relationships, career opportunities, and more. **Unforgiveness can feel like a black hole, swallowing up our destiny, stealing and stalling our purpose.**

It must be said that there is room for the process, here. I am currently, right now, working hard to forgive a few people, people I love, people I'd admired and trusted, people who hurt me. Their offense, at times, feels greater than my ability to ever get over it, and there are moments when I wonder if I will ever stop replaying conversations, mentally listing their wrongs, and building a case in my mind for why they deserve my wrath.

Struggling to forgive and denying that we need to are two different things. One is a pathway to freedom, the other, to bondage and chains.

When I deny my need to forgive, I start to create distance between myself and others, even between myself and God. I begin to take on different identities in different settings based on how safe or unsafe I feel, choosing fear over love. I also start determining who's in and who's out in my life, not based on reality but on the pain of my past. Everyone is suspect. Anything remotely resembling what I have already seen or experienced as bad is out; anything that's good is in. I love a black-and-white faith, because it means I am always right, and since I can justify anything with Scripture, God is always defending my position. There's no room for grey areas, no room for the messy process, no room for the middle or the in-between, and definitely no room for God to disagree with me. I am only focused on what *I will* do according to my vows, not according to Scripture.

The problem is,
what we refuse to forgive,
we become.

In Isaiah 14, the Old Testament prophet Isaiah tells the story of God's redemption as well as his reckoning with the enemy of our souls, the father of lies, and the accuser of humanity, Satan. Satan, who was originally an angel in heaven, glorious and beautiful, fell from his position with God. He was a worship leader turned rock star, obsessed with fame, with glory, with being bigger and better than God. I don't pretend to understand what exactly happened—this story is far above the human pay grade (although scholars definitely have some thoughts—I encourage a good study here), but Satan's language chills me to the bone:

> How you have fallen from heaven,
> morning star, son of the dawn!
> You have been cast down to the earth,
> you who once laid low the nations!
> *You said in your heart,*
> "I will ascend to the heavens;
> I will raise my throne
> above the stars of God;
> I will sit enthroned on the mount of assembly,
> on the utmost heights of Mount Zaphon.
> I will ascend above the tops of the clouds;
> I will make myself like the Most High."
> But you are brought down to the realm of the dead,
> to the depths of the pit.
> (Isa. 14:12–15 NIV, emphasis added)

Oh my, the things I have said in my heart. I'm getting pretty personal with you in this book, but if I told you everything, you'd stop reading. There are things only God knows, and I am forever thankful he refuses to expose and shame me in my weakness. Some secrets make us sick and need to be shared with others for the purpose of our healing and growth, but man, am I glad God is a good secret keeper. He knows our stories, our pain, our sicknesses, and those things we thought (and did) in the dark, and he loves us and chooses us and graces us and blesses us anyway.

Back to Satan. Do you see all those "I will" statements? Now, travel back a bit to the vows I shared with you. Notice any similarities? *I will, I will, I will.* Scripture actually says that I become more like the enemy of my soul, Satan, than the creator and lover of my soul, God, when I tie the beliefs in my heart to pride, hatred, and unforgiveness rather than to humility, love, and forgiveness. I shudder when I consider that I have the capacity to be more like the devil than like God.

———

My husband, Cody, and I met in 2009 and married in 2011. It was literal rainbows and sunshine, one of the happiest times in my life. However, the hurt in my past caused me to struggle during our first year of marriage. I had a very difficult time communicating. I had worked through so many of my issues and learned to live well in deeply connected, open, and honest friendships, but when it came to the most intimate relationship in my life, I felt like there was a muzzle on my mouth. I couldn't open up and share. I would try, but would end up sitting there, saying nothing. I was a stonewaller, and no matter how much I tried to change that, I couldn't. The game changer for me came when Cody sat next to me and said gently, "I know you aren't ready to talk right now, but when you are, I want to hear, and I'll be ready." He treated me the same, loved me, and helped me carry on. Because he didn't condemn me, pick a fight with me, or try to change me, my heart opened up to see God more clearly. Through the tenderness of my husband, I realized God wasn't shaking his finger at me, telling me to get it together, and I began to trust that he wanted to help me and desired to set me free.

As I pressed into God's presence, through the Holy Spirit I felt I heard him say, *You're holding on to unforgiveness, and you have become the thing you hate.* I didn't understand fully what he was trying to tell me, but I did join a weekly eighteen-month recovery group because I realized, even after all I had already overcome, that I still needed healing. Recovery is a lifelong journey, and, in Christ, we are always being made new, so getting some help whenever we need it is necessary.

Step one of recovery is about coming out of denial. As I examined my behavior, I realized I had never fully forgiven an important family member. In their own brokenness, this person was unable to connect. As a child, I would ask questions, and instead of responding, this person would ignore me, no matter how many times I asked. When they were in the room, they were rarely present, mostly aloof, and distant. It hurt me and did significant damage to my perspective on God's presence in my life. I didn't realize I was still holding on to that hurt, and because I was still angry and afraid, I repeated the very thing I feared the most in my marriage. What I vowed I would never become, I was becoming, all because of unforgiveness.

Vows are meant to be a blessing. On our wedding day, my husband and I made vows to one another—until death do us part. We promised to be honest, to be present, to be available in every season. We promised that, whatever our circumstances, we would remain faithful to one another, not just enduring each other but loving and serving whether we felt like it or not. Our vows are rooted in love. I think of my decision to follow Jesus, to give my life to him, to abandon my selfishness in order to see every person as made in the image of God and therefore deserving of acceptance and love, whether I think them worthy or not. I promised to be faithful to Christ, to have no other idol in his place, and though I fail at this often, I strive to let it be so in my life. I promised to live in community with all people, pursuing peace, pursuing wholeness for myself and others, because it is his desire that we would be connected this way. I vowed to think about the greater good, instead of just my own good, for his name's sake. I promised to choose love and not hate. I chose to make these vows to Christ, not because he demanded them or forced me to do so but because no one has ever loved, comforted, or served me better. I love what the apostle Paul, the famous religious leader who stood over Pastor Stephen's body as he was stoned to death and martyred for his love for Christ, says in his letter to his protégé and son in the faith, Timothy:

> This is a trustworthy saying, and everyone should accept it: "Christ Jesus came into the world to save sinners"—and I am the worst of them all. But God had mercy on me so that Christ Jesus could use me as a prime example of his great patience with even the worst sinners. Then others will realize that they, too, can believe in him and receive eternal life. All honor and glory to God forever and ever! He is the eternal King, the unseen one who never dies; he alone is God. Amen. (1 Tim. 1:15–17)

I am the worst of them all. And I am. But God had grace on me. Remembering this, and knowing that I have been and am still forgiven, helps me return to love, return to forgiveness. Because how can I, chief sinner, withhold what I have been given so freely? When we find ourselves splintered, hurting ourselves and hurting others, we can come back to forgiveness. I don't deserve to be forgiven any more than the people I don't want to forgive, but the love of Jesus compels us to release our grip, to free our captors, to forgive those who have sinned against us.

> *Forgiveness makes us whole,*
> *because forgiveness sets us free.*

Freedom is found in forgiveness, the very thing Jesus died to give us. And one by one, he heals our pain, our memories, our addictions and coping mechanisms, our broken hearts and relationships. Experiencing his healing means we don't have to hide. In his presence, there's no need to pretend, no need to give up on our dream or our destiny because we don't feel worthy of love or are ashamed of where we come from. When we've been set free, we don't hurt ourselves or other people, and in Christ we are being made new daily. Our need for a habit that gives us temporary release from our pain is absolved, because our pain has been healed completely. The gap between who we are and who we pretend to be starts closing with forgiveness, because we return to our innocence, our joy, our true self.

But how? How do we forgive, and how do we receive forgiveness? How do we practice this in our daily lives and not just during the huge hurdles of life?

First, we commit ourselves to integrity in our brokenness. Perfection is no longer the goal—being honest is. Honest about our past, honest when we make a mistake, honest when we are wrong, honest in our commitments, careers, and confrontations. What we say is what we mean, and what people see is what people get. Forgiveness comes more easily when we are honest and open with ourselves, with God, and with others.

Second, we confess our reality. Opening up to a safe person (someone who loves us and wants the best for us) about what really happened, and sharing what is happening in real time, are both critical to our wellbeing. We can say, "I don't expect or need you to fix me, save me, advise me, or change me, but this is what I am actually going through, and I do hope you will choose to walk with me and love me anyway." This gives shame a firm kick in the face, and by breaking our silence we are killing our pride and giving the other person an opportunity to show up for us.

Third, we get help. Read a book, find a therapist, join a support group or recovery program, go through a grief and loss class, get in a small group at church. We don't have to lie to live. Freedom is actually possible—if we are willing to put in the work to be free. It's not easy, but we do it because we want to forgive, to be whole, to be free. We choose to show up for our life, every day, and we choose daily to pursue wholeness through forgiveness.

Finally, be a friend and find some friends. The best way to receive and give forgiveness is to practice it with others. When we mess up and our people forgive us, our dignity in the midst of our humanity is affirmed. We recognize that our imperfections and our brokenness are okay. We find a new outlet for our issues and our pain through relationship, and we begin to let go of our destructive habits, addictions, and coping mechanisms. As we receive love and grace from others, we gain a stronger picture of God's love and grace, and as our confidence grows that we are loved as we are, a beautiful thing happens—we decide not to stay there. We grow into our power and purpose, and since we're no longer threatened by others, we help them grow as well.

Forgiveness is powerful. Truth tellers must walk in the freedom of forgiveness, not bitterness, not brokenness, not hopelessness. If we are to rise in strength, then we must rise in forgiveness.

So, what do you say this becomes one of your favorite F-words too?

RISE, *Truth* TELLER

- Our inability to deal with life, face our fears, or sit with the truth means we will settle for living a hidden or masked existence.
- Forgiveness leads to wholeness.
- Unforgiveness can feel like a black hole, swallowing up our destiny, stealing and stalling our purpose.
- Struggling to forgive and denying that we need to are two different things. One is a pathway to freedom, the other to bondage and chains.
- What we refuse to forgive, we become.
- Forgiveness makes us whole, because forgiveness sets us free.

TELL THE *Truth*

- So, got any good F-word stories?
- Had you ever thought about forgiveness's connection to wholeness?
- What vows have you made because of the hurts in your past? How have they hindered you from living honestly and vulnerably? Have they affected your pursuit of your purpose?
- How has unforgiveness stopped you from trusting? From loving? From serving?
- Read Colossians 3:13–15. What stands out to you? Think about your actions toward others and their actions toward you. Are your actions congruent with these verses? Is there anything you would do differently?

three

THE TRUTH ABOUT PROCESS

Seriously, Are We Still Dealing with This?

> Hi, my name is Ashley. I am a grateful believer in
> Jesus Christ who struggles with pride, control, and
> anger.

As forgiveness becomes a daily practice, a natural rhythm of
our life with God, we begin to reckon with the words abiding
on the inside of our souls. We have to face the fears lying beneath the surface that we often expend energy trying to deny,
run from, or wallow in.

I am tired and I am alone.

These words bang around my brain relentlessly when I'm
hurting—two thoughts that have burrowed in my belly, rest-
less within me, as long as I can remember. People often talk

about the vicious cycle of guilt and shame, but for me, *tired* and *alone* is my endless yo-yo. Feeling alone in any struggle makes me tired, and when I am tired, isolation soon follows. I don't know which comes first, but they are both ever-present in my body.

That's where I feel things. I respond with my gut, I store stress in my neck and back, I keep emotions and exhaustion pent up inside my body. My first instinct is to act, to move, to do something. If anger is the emotion, I am moved to want to throat-punch someone. If compassion stirs my heart, I am moved to meet the need in front of me. If love is the feeling, I am moved to show affection. When something's not right, I feel it in my body; my muscles tense, my legs stiffen, and I prepare myself to act. When a person is unsafe and I sense danger, the hair on the back of my neck rises and a sense of dread fills my stomach. The opposite is true as well. When something is right, I feel my body relax and I more easily release the pressure to protect, pretend, or perform.

My body is my first truth teller.

Sometimes, I want to hug myself in the fetal position because I have spent so much of my life resisting my own body, ignoring her warning signs, giving people and situations more time, effort, and energy than they deserved, risking my heart, soul, body, future, and talents, all because I didn't listen to myself. Even in my brokenness, the times when I've been wrong or judged someone prematurely, my body would still respond appropriately, and most of the time, if I was willing to work through the fear, I'd find myself in spaces and with people I loved.

I've got a pretty hilarious example of "Ashley doesn't listen to her gut and almost misses a really good thing." It's my husband. Guys, first of all, he's from Texas.

For those of you who live in the great state of Texas, or hail from 'round those parts, I apologize in advance, but you have quite a reputation in the media. And prior to 2010, well, I'd only ever flown into your Dallas airport. (Which is lovely, by the way. I have a special affection for your large red chairs, many Starbucks options, and, as a mom, your breastfeeding room and play area for children. You surely are superior in these ways. I understand that this is how you like it, and so I am giving honor where it is due.)

From the big hair, to the wild and sometimes scandalous religious and political leaders, to Waco pre–Joanna Gaines, to the extra-conservative values, to the passion for the NRA, and to the reportedly staunch immigration policies, I figured Texas was not really a place that would be too accepting of a serious wild woman like me, so I really had no interest in spending time there. (However, with the wild mane on my head I look like a stereotypical Texan, so there is absolutely no reason "big hair" should have made my list.)

Well, the Lord works in mysterious ways, because a car accident changed everything. I was driving like a maniac down Wilshire Boulevard, Los Angeles, with one of my best friends, Katherine, in the passenger seat, and when I changed lanes I definitely did not check my blind spot and body-slammed another vehicle. Everything but the bodies of the cars and our necks were okay, so we carried on with our plan to go to church, which was just down the street from the incident.

My future husband, Cody, and I were serving in the choir together, but we didn't really know each other. He was creative, kind, and fun, but not on my radar. He did not fit some items on my ridiculous "future husband needs to have/be/do" list. (Sidenote, I should have burned that list. Because, really, who does that? Who makes a list of all the things a human should be before they get to be with me? Who dooms themselves from the start with false expectations and certain disappointment? Apparently, lots of girls in church, because everyone I knew had a dumb list, and usually also a specific dude "God had told them was their husband" in mind. Who is teaching us this garbage? Also, for the love of biblical accuracy, that is not what Habakkuk meant when he said, "Write the vision and make it plain." While I'm on this soapbox, he cried out and acted for the good of the people, not for his personal ten-year goal strategy, and communal repentance and transformation were required, not individualism, materialism, and consumerism.)

So, anyway, Cody didn't seem to fit my list; plus he was from Texas, which meant that he must be a good ol' boy, bless God, the holiest of holies. My fear of ending up in a relationship where I was not valued for who I was, for what I was created to contribute, or where I would be coerced to sit pretty and stay silent was real. I am from a long lineage of spitting, kicking, say what you think, and don't tell me what to do kind of women. What sort of marriage would I have with someone who wanted me to "act right"? *Do you see how crazy this sounds?* I didn't even know the man and I had already decided that we couldn't possibly be good together. Look at all the judgments I'd made based on the broad strokes of media I'd digested, the weird church culture of spouse picking, and my own personal fears!

Fear and the culture we're immersed in give us plenty of opportunities to rise in the wrong truth, but God is patient and gives us grace.

Plus, Cody was just so good-looking. Like, what was wrong with him? Why did he look like someone carved him like a statue? How did he have such big lips? Was he seriously always in that good of a mood? *Who is this man?*

The night of the accident, after church, Cody offered to walk me to my car with a few of my friends. When we got to the gate, he placed his hand on the small of my back and wanted to know if I needed anything before I left to take my car to the mechanic. I said no, but thanks for asking, and we said goodbye.

Standing in the parking lot next to me as we watched him go, another of my best friends, Harmony, stared at me with her jaw on the ground.

"Ashley, what's up with Cody Abercrombie?"

Clueless, per usual, I responded, "Cody? Nothing is up with Cody Abercrombie."

She could not even find enough eyes to roll. "Girl, he put his hand on you, and you didn't even flinch! Something's up with Cody Abercrombie." And then she smirked and said loudly, "Mmm hmmm."

All the way home, I kept thinking about it. *I didn't even flinch. Huh! That's crazy! Wait, do I like Cody? Like, like him, like him? What is happening? How is this possible? He's from Texas! He went to school in Waco pre–Fixer Upper!*

My mind held a few "facts" but my body told the truth. Texan as he was, he was good to the core, and when he called me up, like a boss, and said, "Here's the deal, Ashley: I really like you, and I'd like to get to know you better. Can I take you on a date?" you're doggone right I said, "Yes! I would love to!" And then squealed like a little girl, jumping up and down in a corporate lunchroom.

I knew for certain he would be my husband when I felt like a ball of fire as his elbow grazed my arm, and I thought for sure we would never make it to marriage without a desperate need for forgiveness. I blushed so bad I thought I'd die, and even though I didn't tell him at the time, I knew it was signed, sealed, delivered. Game over. Turnt like a turnip.

In the good, the bad, and the ugly, my body tells no lies.

Still, when I feel tired and alone, I tend to ignore or bury what I know is true. Standing before the potential for real love and companionship, I needed friends to see what I couldn't. My fears and judgments were louder than the movement of God in front of me. Do you deal with this too? The struggle to own the truth, to push past the pain of the past and enter the necessary process of transformation?

When my heart is aching from my need for connection, my body screaming for solitude, my mind running in a hurry, I still find myself choosing to stay busy, distracted, and disconnected anyway. It's so much easier to work overtime, scroll through social media, stay up on current events, or worry about everyone and everything else than it is to take responsibility for my soul and deal with what's lurking beneath the surface through a daily process of taking inventory that involves reflection and relationship.

Owning our stories and rising in truth is a process.

It does not happen overnight, no matter how many books we read, TED Talks we watch, or podcasts we hear; true transformation takes time. After trying all the "instant change" remedies on God's green earth, I've grown in my capacity to allow time to do its thing and have even come to love the process. The word *process* as a noun means a systematic series of actions directed to some end; a continuous action, operation, or series of changes taking place in a definite matter; the whole course of the proceedings in an action at law; the action of going forward or on; the condition of being carried on. As a verb it means to treat or prepare by some particular series of actions, as in manufacturing; to require (someone) to answer questionnaires, perform various tasks, and sometimes to undergo physical and aptitude classification examinations before the beginning or termination of a period of service; to serve a process or summons on. The word has its roots in the Middle English word *proces* (noun) and the Latin word *processus*, which both mean "a going forward" with a variant stem of the word *cedere*, which means "to yield." When it has the suffix *-tus* attached in its verb form, "action" is the added definition.*

Which explains my fundamental problem with process: it is a going forward in which I must manage the constant tension of yielding and taking action. Process implies both a surrender to time and an acceptance of responsibility. I have little control over the time the process takes, and I can only do my part to own my stuff and stop blaming others. I cannot hurry healing or quickly brush past my history or my present moment,

*Dictionary.com, s.v. "process," http://www.dictionary.com/browse/process.

and the accompanying anxiety, disappointment, heartbreak, or whatever else might be nagging me to deal with it. Denial will not quicken the process. ("I'm fine, just fine. Everything's fine.") Neither will relying on my coping mechanisms, yo-yoing between restraint and indulgence. Food, drugs, alcohol, men, and achievements may help us live with the pain but they will not heal it.

Believe me, I've tried that list and then some.

That's why I like ignoring the pain, all that stuff lurking beneath the surface of my daily life and responsibilities, because who has time to actually slow down and deal with that? Living in reality is really, really hard. Actually, living in reality with hopeful expectation is hard. Reality is kind of easy if you can grumble and complain about it and build a whole identity on how tired, busy, annoyed, and angry you are. But to accept what is and to live with hope for what will or could be, or make choices instead of excuses, now that is a serious challenge.

Before experiencing real freedom in my life in relationship with Christ, I actually thought that living without the pain of my past was impossible and addiction would always be my way of dealing with life. ("Hello, my name is Ashley, and I am a prideful, controlling, angry addict.") After saying yes to following Jesus, I thought I would arrive at this euphoria of being utterly unbothered and free of issues, problems, and pain. I thought the magic pill of salvation was about not only fixing things for good but also making me (and my life) perfect.

Then I realized that's probably some other religion.

The Bible is full of hardcore, devoted-unto-death lovers of God and followers of Jesus, men and women who were stoned, imprisoned, beaten, abandoned, rejected, or martyred and made other unimaginable sacrifices. But to be honest, the triumphant, romanticized, sanitized, whitewashed victory stories I heard in church for most of my adult life focused so much on the outcomes—and nearly always the wins—that I missed the process. I missed the cost. I missed the pain. I missed the time that it takes to see something good come from struggle.

I was in for a rude awakening when I realized how often I was waiting for a win and that perfection in the Bible was about me becoming whole, by becoming more like Christ, and not about me creating and controlling the narrative for my perfect, triumphant, and victorious life.

The "name it and claim it" culture is fabulous. Everything is in a hurry and very black-and-white: "God, I claim that you will do this, and it will be done because I have declared it." It is shouting down healing, providence, provision, deliverance, and freedom—and expecting it to come and come right now, without hard work, patience, perseverance, or struggle. Oh yes, I am here for the black-and-white, formulaic faith, honey. Grey space is for the birds.

But I always find God in the grey, at the margins of my certainty, at the end of my unfulfilled, arrogant declarations.

Who am I to tell God anything about what he should do? Yes, God is good and God does good, but for the love of all things sacred and holy, he is Creator of heaven and earth, the King of kings and Lord of lords, holy and perfect in all his ways. And while he encourages us throughout Scripture to call on his name, ask for what we need, and pray in line with his Word, I see no passage that gives me—a tiny human, a vapor in light of eternity, a member of the human community made holy only by the blood of Jesus—permission to tell God what he ought to be doing. So we can do our best to resist naming and claiming anything, except that which is written in his Word, and even then we must remind ourselves that if God doesn't do it, and if he doesn't come through for us (because let's face the facts: sometimes he doesn't do what we ask)—even then, especially then, we must choose to give him praise. Our devotion cannot be dependent on our personal happiness or our levels of satisfaction but on our trust and sacrifice. *If I lose everything, even my life, I will still trust you.*

In that place, when we are finally willing to relinquish control and more readily admit that the illusion of security we've imagined for ourselves is the lesser version of faith, we discover God, in his mystery and chaos, asking us to accept what is and to trust, surrender, and obey. Surrender is the critical posture in the process. No time limits, no striving to achieve, no fixing it all the way we think it should be fixed, no manipulating or controlling to impact outcomes, no blaming and shaming others so we can wallow in what we don't have the courage to change. Surrender. Be present right now, doing the best we can where we are with what we have in our process of transformation. John Ortberg, pastor and author of *Soul Keeping*, asked his mentor, the late theologian Dallas Willard, what he could do to remain spiritually healthy in the midst of all he had going on. Dallas responded:

"You must ruthlessly eliminate hurry from your life." [*]

Ugh, but hurry is what I do best! Can I get a witness? I rush from here to there, moving as quickly as possible from

---

[*]John Ortberg, *Soul Keeping: Caring for the Most Important Part of You* (Grand Rapids: Zondervan, 2014), 20.

one thing to the next, hustling in my career, my healing, my relationships; running uphill all the time; and hurrying God along like he's a toddler I am dragging through the crosswalk. It's embarrassing, frankly.

———

Back when tiny humans didn't interrupt my Bible time with demands, I used to journal. Like with an actual pen and paper. (Not with my phone on the toilet for two minutes begging God to speak and speak quickly, in Jesus's name, amen.) Sometimes, as I pored over Scripture, a picture would come alive in my heart and mind that I would try to capture on the page. One day during my journal time, God gently began to push me to face the two deepest pain points in my soul: *tired* and *alone*. I saw myself hustling, running, and striving, doing my best to climb up a mountain. There was no one with me. I had a flag in my hand and sheer exhaustion was on my face and in my body, but I was committed to getting to the top of that mountain, no matter what it cost me.

As I journaled, I read Isaiah 30—and no, I don't know why God would send someone just getting to know him to the book of Isaiah, but it worked for me.

> Now go and write down these words.
>   Write them in a book.
> They will stand until the end of time
>   as a witness
> that these people are stubborn rebels
>   who refuse to pay attention to the LORD's
>   instructions.
> *They tell the seers,*
>   *"Stop seeing visions!"*

They tell the prophets,
  "Don't tell us what is right.
Tell us nice things.
  Tell us lies.
Forget all this gloom.
  Get off your narrow path.
Stop telling us about your
  'Holy One of Israel.'"
This is the reply of the Holy One of Israel:
"Because you despise what I tell you
  and trust instead in oppression and lies,
calamity will come upon you suddenly—
  like a bulging wall that bursts and falls.
In an instant it will collapse
  and come crashing down.
You will be smashed like a piece of pottery—
  shattered so completely that
there won't be a piece big enough
  to carry coals from a fireplace
  or a little water from the well."
This is what the Sovereign Lord,
  the Holy One of Israel, says:
"Only in returning to me
  and resting in me will you be saved.
In quietness and confidence is your strength.
  But you would have none of it.
You said, 'No, we will get our help from Egypt.
  They will give us swift horses for riding into battle.'
But the only swiftness you are going to see
  is the swiftness of your enemies chasing you!
One of them will chase a thousand of you.
  Five of them will make all of you flee.

You will be left like a lonely flagpole on a hill
 or a tattered banner on a distant mountaintop."
So the Lord *must wait for you to come to him*
 so he can show you his love and compassion.
For the Lord *is a faithful God.*
 Blessed are those who wait for his help.
O people of Zion, who live in Jerusalem,
 you will weep no more.
He will be gracious if you ask for help.
 He will surely respond to the sound of your cries.
Though the Lord gave you adversity for food
 and suffering for drink,
he will still be with you to teach you.
 You will see your teacher with your own eyes.
Your own ears will hear him.
 Right behind you a voice will say,
"This is the way you should go,"
 whether to the right or to the left.
Then you will destroy all your silver idols
 and your precious gold images.
You will throw them out like filthy rags,
 saying to them, "Good riddance!"

Then the Lord will bless you with rain at planting time. There will be wonderful harvests and plenty of pastureland for your livestock. The oxen and donkeys that till the ground will eat good grain, its chaff blown away by the wind. *In that day, when your enemies are slaughtered and the towers fall, there will be streams of water flowing down every mountain and hill. The moon will be as bright as the sun, and the sun will be seven times brighter—like the light of seven days in one! So it will be when the* Lord *begins to heal his people and cure the wounds he gave them.* (Isa. 30:8–26, emphasis added)

All right, some of you are likely wondering what in the world you just read, and I apologize, but by now you can clearly see that I am a strange bird and my passion for Old Testament prophets is the least of my problems, so I hope you'll hang in there as we go through these verses in Isaiah. God used this passage, and is still using it, to help me see myself as I really am, because my tendency to live exhausted and isolated is still a struggle. Better than it used to be, by far, but *tired* and *alone* remain present nonetheless. I thought I'd take you through my process of reading Scripture and letting it affect me in the hopes that it will affect you too.

From my experience, I can say Bible reading can be a challenge for most people. No one really talks about that in church, where we hear about these magical quiet times through the lens of people who are pastors and teachers and primarily connect with God through the written word because they are gifted to teach it. In reality, after fifteen years of ministry experience, I have rarely met a person, including myself, who reads their Bible faithfully every single day. When people feel safe to share, they often reveal that "quiet time" is something they feel guilty about not doing rather than something that they do. We must remember that there is no shortage of ways to experience the Holy Spirit (serving others, worship, solitude, fasting, celebration, prayer, nature, community, advocacy), and as individuals we can discover our unique pathways to God. At the same time, we must develop a consistent habit of reading and listening to the Bible, because it is a primary way we read and hear wisdom, gain understanding, and integrate that into our daily practices.

The Bible keeps us faithful to Christ in a digital world of social media where our mind and soul are often fed by sound bites, clever quips that lack context, and phrases that preach well but don't always live well. We need to seek the truth of God for ourselves, because we can't survive on somebody else's sermon. We must allow him to be our first teacher as we use our minds, engage our hearts, and open our lives up for transformation.

Isaiah 30 was one of those revelatory moments in life when I finally understood truth. I didn't just gain wisdom from God; he gave me understanding about the deeply rooted issues in my soul and his solutions for me to find help and healing. There is no way on earth that this passage would have made sense to me outside of my spending time reading, reflecting, and asking God for help with being so tired and feeling alone. I read it several times and paid attention to the phrases and words that stood out to me.

> They tell the seers,
>   "Stop seeing visions!"
> They tell the prophets,
>   "Don't tell us what is right.
> Tell us nice things.
>   Tell us lies.
> Forget all this gloom.
>   Get off your narrow path.
> Stop telling us about your
>   'Holy One of Israel.'" (vv. 10–11)

Oh, man. Busted. This is exactly what I want to hear every time I go to the Word. Nice things. I want to hear that the way I'm living is somehow okay, that if I go along with culture it's fine. But what I learn here is that I am likely resisting the very painful path of change. That I'm in the wrong struggle, running down the wide road of anxiety, stress, loneliness, and isolation. That if I'm not careful, I have a tendency to isolate Scriptures to suit my lifestyle so I feel good rather than interpreting their true context and meaning so I can be transformed into the image and integrity of God. Because the truth is that me being and/or feeling tired and alone is often a result of the choices I make about how to live my life. It's tough to hear that, so, like those in the beginning of this passage, I feel tempted to silence the truth tellers around me, asking them to tell me everything's fine instead of reminding me that I've isolated myself or that I'm doing too much too fast. I'm faced with the truth that fear and self-sufficiency are at the root of my relationship issues.

> This is the reply of the Holy One of Israel:
> "Because you despise what I tell you
>   and trust instead in oppression and lies,
> calamity will come upon you suddenly—
>   like a bulging wall that bursts and falls.
> In an instant it will collapse
>   and come crashing down." (vv. 12–13)

I learn here that I've been despising God's wisdom and trusting in oppression and lies. Fear of failure and never being good enough is actually what's chasing me up the mountain, not God. Living under this taskmaster, who I happen to have been calling "God," is beating me half to death, and my need to strive, achieve, and pioneer is actually what's killing me. Here I learn the falseness of my belief that if I am to make something of myself, I have to do it all by myself. This whole thing I've been building in order to feel significant is about to come crashing down like a house of cards.

This is what the Sovereign LORD,
   the Holy One of Israel, says:
"Only in returning to me
   and resting in me will you be saved.
In quietness and confidence is your strength.
   But you would have none of it. . . .
You will be left like a lonely flagpole on a hill
   or a tattered banner on a distant mountaintop."
     (vv. 15, 17)

Here is where God gives me the solution to the issues of being tired and feeling alone: *returning* and *resting*. Repentance and rest will save me. And he plainly lays out the truth of what my life might be if I insist that my way is better: "You will be left like a lonely flagpole on a hill, or a tattered banner on a distant mountaintop" (v. 17). This sits in me like a painful reality and at the same time sets me free. *I don't have to live this way—what a relief!* I am not alone. God is with me. God is with you. He has created us to live in communion with him and with each other. Striving to achieve, to make a name for myself is not his highest and best. I am significant no matter my circumstances. I am someone even without any relational attachments or personal achievements. My value and dignity are inherent in the God who made me. I bear his image. I do not have to exhaust myself to please him or anybody else. And neither do you. We are significant. We are someone. We are the image of God on the earth. We don't have to prove ourselves.

We are loved exactly as we are, all the way through every single process of growth and change.

The goal of the process is *wholeness*: to live with integrity and strength, integrated in relationship with God and others, pursuing a life worth living because it is richly connected to something bigger than itself. Process helps us take inventory of who we are becoming, not just what we are doing, and it presses us to eliminate hurry.

> So the LORD must wait for you to come to him
> so he can show you his love and compassion.
> For the LORD is a faithful God.
> Blessed are those who wait for his help. (v. 18)

The Lord is ever patient, merciful, faithful, and full of grace. He will never leave you, no matter what you have done and no matter what your deepest, darkest secrets and issues are. He sees your need and is actively and always choosing you, whether you are at your best or your worst.

He waits with love for us to come to him, to humble ourselves, to admit that we need him, that our self-sufficiency, our anxiety and fear, our taskmasters of the soul are no longer working for us. Return. Repent. Wait. Rest. He will help you, beloved.

RISE, *Truth* TELLER

- Owning our stories and rising in truth is a process.
- Food, drugs, alcohol, men, and achievements may help us live with the pain but they will not heal it.
- We must ruthlessly eliminate hurry from our life.
- We are loved exactly as we are, all the way through every single process of growth and change.

- We are significant. We are someone. We are the image of God on the earth.
- Return. Repent. Wait. Rest.

TELL THE *Truth*

- What are the deeper fears lurking beneath the surface of your veneer?
- What is your first indicator that something is right or wrong?
- Are there any wrong truths you've believed and risen in? How did they impact your choices and the lives of the people around you?
- Remember my Texas story? How has the culture around you (church, media and entertainment, family structure) impacted your sense of judgment?
- What do you think of the Dallas Willard quote? How do you resist living life in a hurry?

four

THE TRUTH ABOUT TRAUMA

Wait, This Isn't Normal?

Though he slay me, yet will I trust in him.

Job 13:15 KJV

Budgeting and dealing with trauma really should be required in school, and also should be a parenting prerequisite, because those are actual life skills we need. I don't know about you, but Lord knows I didn't use words like *trauma* growing up. Most of us don't have the language we desperately need to share the impact of words, abuse, pain, and circumstances on our hearts, minds, and bodies. We just get through it and manage it the best way we know how. If that means suppressing or ignoring, addicting or perfecting, we do it, because at least we're surviving.

Recently I began to read books on childhood development to close my own information and experience gap, to better understand how my children are processing the world around them, and to assist in their healthy emotional and mental growth. My capacity to teach, remain present, and care for them, especially when they are dealing with the big emotions, is limited. The most helpful resource I've read so far is a book called *The Whole Brain Child: 12 Revolutionary Strategies to Help Nurture Your Child's Developing Mind*, by Daniel J. Siegel and Tina Payne Bryson.

The authors discuss the power of integration of the brain (left and right, upstairs and downstairs) for health and success in order to help parents not just survive in parenting but thrive. They use powerful imagery that sticks and phrases I can remember, and even though the book isn't based on the Bible, the science confirms what I know to be true in both my relationship with God and my recovery journey.

One of the profound, simple sentences the authors use is "Name it to tame it."[*]

How sticky is this phrase? Too often, we ourselves "dismiss and deny" the emotional experience of life's events, and we spend a great deal of time talking ourselves—and our children—out of our emotions, using logic to skip over the feelings. We want to move on quickly instead of stopping to deal with the issue. For example, we think we're helping our children come out of their big, scary emotions by telling them it's not that bad or distracting them with something else, but in

---

[*]Daniel J. Siegel and Tina Payne Bryson, *The Whole Brain Child: 12 Revolutionary Strategies to Help Nurture Your Child's Developing Mind* (New York: Bantam, 2012), Kindle ed., chapter 2.

reality, we unknowingly disconnect and refuse to acknowledge what they're facing. And I don't know if you've ever tried to rush a toddler who is thrashing on the floor and refusing socks and shoes because there was not enough time to make a smooth transition, but if you have, you know the toddler will not be rushed and nothing really helps except slowing down and giving them time to process. Just like us, when children are forced to stuff their natural emotions and fears somewhere else, they learn to operate in the world in a way that may not be healthy or helpful for their emotional wellbeing. (And yes, I feel you. I just want them to put their shoes on without an intense showdown. Unfortunately, screaming, forcing, and controlling have a temporary effect that suits our momentary agenda but also a long-term effect that impacts their functional capacity and way of being in the world.)

In order to tame the big, overwhelming feelings, we have to name them through a process of storytelling. The writers encourage us to listen to the story our child is sharing (even if they are only old enough to point and share a word or two at a time) and make sense of it with the child so that they can process the raging sea of emotions and be released from fear.* Let the kids share in their own way and help them tell the story. Ask questions: What happened next? And did you remember when? And then what did you do? This helps the memory become less scary and gives them the internal capacity to deal with the incident without burying it or covering it with other distractions. Talking about it frees them from fear and insecurity and gives them a way of sharing and dealing with issues and incidents.

*Siegel and Bryson, *The Whole Brain Child*, chapter 2.

This is true in my own life. Every time I have been given safe space to share the whole truth, without judgment, I have experienced immediate relief and healing.

My first relapse with bulimia was after an incredible weekend. I was six months or so sober from bulimia and spent a few days serving at a conference in another city. What I didn't realize about recovery at the time is that the highs have to be managed just as much as the lows. I didn't pay attention to how tired I was or how much emotional energy I'd expended. When I stepped back into my apartment, where I was alone, I didn't expect the crash in emotions after the high of the event and didn't yet have the tools to reach out and to process, and so, I relapsed.

What saved me was storytelling. Terrified, I took a risk and found the courage to share with a few friends exactly what had happened. And it was messy—I am not even sure I made any sense (just like my kids when they are raging), but my friends were an incredible mirror for me, asking questions just like the ones above, helping me tell my story so that I could identify where things started to get offtrack. With their understanding, I began to piece together what happened (name it to tame it). I was vulnerable because I had been surrounded by others in a faith community and then suddenly alone for a few days. I also was off my schedule, the established routine that helped me stick to sobriety, and I had been unable to eat the healthy foods I knew nourished my body. It took its toll on the back end, but with my friends' help, a new fact dropped from the knowledge in my head down into the wisdom of my heart: one relapse didn't mean my whole recovery journey was shot. It only meant that sometimes I made mistakes.

Perfection is not the goal; wholeness is.

Overall, I was in a really good place. What we do in a weak moment, what we feel on our recovery journey, is not who we are. Without my friends' perspectives, I would have ignored the fact that I had been sober from drugs, alcohol, and bulimia for six whole months! My one mistake felt like a stain on my recovery, and I deeply feared that this meant I was incapable of being completely free. Eating disorders are incredibly difficult to recover from because we need to eat to live. But my friends helped me see the white, open page of healing rather than focus solely on that one dot on the timeline of my recovery. Isn't it funny how one moment can eclipse days and weeks and months of hard work?

Storytelling within the context of healthy relationships, with safe people we love, is mission critical for dealing with trauma.

Yes, and amen to counseling, therapy, group therapy, recovery, spiritual direction, classes, mentorship, and serving. But without friends to see us at our worst, to show up for us in our mess, it is difficult to feel fully loved as we are. We need people who will be present in our pain and not try to fix us, save us, or advise us. Because that's who God is. He practices the ministry of presence, and he does not grow tired or weary of us. He does not read a boundary book and decide to cut us out of his life because we cannot get it together. He's a perfect father, and his love is unconditional whether we change or not, and this fact is the very thing that frees us and gives us grace to change. He knows we need to be loved first, not after we meet all his standards.

With a few people in our lives to love us like this (few is for real, y'all—we don't need twenty homies, just two or three), we experience the fullness of God's love in the fullness of our relationships with others who are willing to love us like God does. The ideology that says "It's just me and Jesus, because I don't need or like people" is a bunch of bull hockey. I know we've all been hurt and that's why we develop this mentality, but how is that really working for us?

Being loved where we are, without expectations and conditions, is the only thing powerful enough to make us stop letting life happen to us and instead take ownership over our responsibilities and choices. Love is gentle but firm enough to command that we get up. That we try again, that we change, that we forgive and let go and recover. Striving doesn't do that. Bitterness doesn't do that. Hatred won't do that. Those things sure will keep you working hard but hardly working, as they say in the South. And listen to me, sister; the devil is busy. He will have us wanting things from people we don't even like, performing and pretending for people who have no intention of ever giving us their approval, risking it all for accolades from people we don't even know, lying on Instagram for likes—with no one to call when it's three o'clock in the morning and we are completely falling apart.

The truth about trauma is that it's impossible.
Unbearable. Unbelievable.

If we don't deal with it, we need constant numbing to put it down. We repeat the trauma through poor relationship choices; we spend hours on social media and entertainment; we eat, drink, or work around the clock; we avoid, suppress, and self-harm. And then we go and watch more of it on television, trying to put a Band-Aid over a bullet hole.

At the same time, suffering is also sacred, a gift to our humanity. The beautiful glow of a person passing from this life into eternity. The tears of a mother in mourning who is choosing to go on. A child who laughs in the middle of a painful loss. A couple faced with the difficulty of infertility, deciding again to trust and believe. The right decision for integrity that costs a person everything. These moments are sacred because they must be done. They must be endured. Our suffering is sacred to God.

We know suffering well, don't we? Being human is hard.

I have sat at the bedside of my dying stepmom, her body shredded from eight years of breast cancer coming and going throughout her entire body, a tube inserted into a three-inch hole in her side the only way she could relieve herself. I've sat by my beloved Grandpa Dodson as he refused to eat, so tired that he shriveled himself down to death because he did not want to die at home, so my grandmother would be able to remain in the house they built. I've visited a young teenage girl lying in a hospital bed, her face lit with joy as she died from leukemia. I drove a beautiful woman to a health clinic in Tijuana as a final hope for healing from stage five breast cancer, but she died not even a week later.

I have officiated funerals for stillborn babies, memorial services for women wanting closure for aborted children, and the funeral service for a dear friend's mother. How do you help your friend say goodbye to her mother? I have stood next to the grave of my baby brother and delivered the funeral message for my grandma, who was buried next to him. Because my mom's mother passed away at New Year's during our first year living in New York, I did not have the money to fly home and be with Mama, and my heart still aches from not holding her hand and encouraging her as she made difficult decisions for the family.

I have personally witnessed trauma and tragedy and worked to fight systemic injustice in homeless shelters, impoverished neighborhoods, jail cells, and government housing, and it has caused me to ask difficult questions about my faith. What I understood about the good news of the gospel, and about the very formation of my entire belief system, is that all my Christian clichés and invitations to church just don't hold up in these spaces.

Faith has to grow in suffering. There are no easy answers, no firm ways forward, no instant outcomes.

Unintentionally playing church, building a brand, and having a cool sound board and worship team can't satisfy the ache and longing of humanity. Celebrating the victory of Christ without leaving room for grief, loss, mourning, and lament feels arrogant and isolating to the very people I desperately want to serve. I had to recognize how naïve and insular my faith had become. I had to realize that hosting services and programs that were sometimes out of touch with people's lived reality felt incredibly inadequate in the face of so much suffering. I'd failed to grasp that the Lord never healed anyone the same way twice, that he brought his presence before he brought his ideologies and advice, and that I hadn't one time read about Jesus inviting anyone to the temple. His idea of evangelism and compassion is very different from how we've believed. He doesn't just care about our individual salvation but the way we operate in community as well.

The Christian faith is communal, not just personal, and how we treat each other, the way we decide who's in and who's out, and what we are inviting people into matters to God. I started to resent the pyramid style of leadership I saw at work in the church and began to feel like all of our decisions were made for us before we ever even arrived. Those at the top were the elite vision carriers, and everyone else existed to fulfill their vision, which we did not get to contribute toward, and to invite others to come help us do their bidding. The table had already been set, without our input, but we could add more chairs. To the leadership, that meant we were equitable and inclusive.

What we really were was biased and exclusive, with control as our highest value.

I didn't see this in the life of Jesus. My trust in the evangelical church as an institution eroded, especially as I immersed myself into other cultures where collaboration and shared goals were key to moving a vision forward. As I began to cry out to God with my belief system falling apart, fully awake and alive to suffering in my own life and in the lives of others within and outside of the church, he began to show me another way.

Through Scripture, I saw that Jesus preached with passion and fervor and spoke truth to power, letting the religious leaders know that their elitism and favoritism were the exact opposite of godly, even though it would eventually cost him his life. He disrupted the status quo, and his leadership style was transcendental, not transactional. He gave us free will, operating in humility and seeking transformation, not power and control, even though he had both of those things. In the city, he kneeled. He prayed. He healed. He lifted and shifted, dignified and qualified. He called, corrected, kept, and sent his people. He loved the unlovable, and my God, my precious Jesus, went to battle against physical and sexual violence because he saw daughters and sisters and mothers, young boys and men, and he restored their place.

I started asking questions about church—*God, is this what you had in mind? Is this your best? Is this what I want to spend my life building?* Grief nearly overcame my heart. It was so scary to think about leaving something I had spent years building, to admit that I desired something more meaningful for my life and I wanted to pursue a more just society in the way of Jesus much more than I wanted to attend Sunday services with leaders who wanted me to build their thing. As long as I was doing the most, I was esteemed and given access to personal relationships with leadership, but when I raised questions and concerns, I was silenced and pushed out. The trauma of that transition, combined with my changing belief system about the church and my faith not working everywhere I took it, shook my foundation. And it kept shaking, until everything that could be shaken was shaken, and what could not be shaken was the only thing that remained. And it sure wasn't much.

I didn't leave the church I'd attended, served, and helped build for almost fifteen years with speaking gigs or book deals or any platform or pastor to release me. All I had was my family, friends, and a knowing that I had to walk away. Integrity cost me connection. But God had been building in me trust and character to sustain me. He showed me what was right for me, and I had to follow him. Friend, have you been there? In the grey space of church? Unsure if you want to be there but terrified to leave? Or perhaps you've been kicked out, left out, or laid out as collateral damage by the spiritual leadership in your life.

There is hope for you, hope for us, hope for the church.

The Lord settled my heart with his Word, and I pray this passage will also bless you if you are aching in trauma, lacking real community, or struggling with the church.

> He has shown you, O man, what *is* good;
> and what does the LORD require of you
> But to do justly,
> To love mercy,
> And to walk humbly with your God? (Micah 6:8
> NKJV)

Justice, mercy, and humility with God and with others. This is what is good. For me, the conviction to live this way was so strong that I could no longer live in a way that contradicted it. As I walked away, it felt as though nearly everything in my life was dying. But the truth is, I also felt alive again, awake, present to the pain of others in the same way the Lord had been present to me. I was comfortable with my own brokenness and found myself ready to give grace to the systems and structures I had believed in but were no longer working for me.

Great gain means great loss.

We must continuously let go of the narrow, religious, controlling (easy) gospel that serves us so well in order to inherit a Spirit-filled, compassionate, albeit difficult one. Suffering is a gift, and in all the grief and loss we discover Emmanuel, God with us, One who is neither aloof nor apathetic to our pain but present, awake, and available to us. In trauma, we live in uncertainty with unresolved tension, but the silver lining is that all we have is *right now*. With the present as our sole focus, we live like our Savior, who willingly accepted the hand he was dealt and still went about doing good, unencumbered by the weight of this troubling and disturbing world.

> So Satan went out from the presence of the LORD and afflicted Job with painful sores from the soles of his feet to the crown of his head. Then Job took a piece of broken pottery and scraped himself with it as he sat among the ashes. His wife said to him, "Are you still maintaining your integrity? Curse God and die!" He replied, "You are talking like a foolish woman. Shall we accept good from God, and not trouble?" In all this, Job did not sin in what he said. (Job 2:7–10 NIV)

Weep, dear friend; grieve and mourn over the pain and trauma in your life, in the lives of others, in the city, and in the church, but do not curse God. Shall you and I accept only good from God and not trouble? **Is our obedience limited by our understanding, or shall we trust him in the chaos and the fire?**

> And everything I've taught you is so that the peace which is in me will be in you and will give you great confidence as you rest in me. For in this unbelieving world you will experience trouble and sorrows, but you must be courageous, for I have conquered the world! (John 16:33 TPT)

Surrender, trust, and obey. Accept what is and remember what will be in Christ and the coming kingdom. What we see is not all there is to see. Now rise from the ashes, sister. Begin again anew.

RISE, *Truth* TELLER

- "Name it to tame it."
- Perfection is not the goal; wholeness is.
- Storytelling within the context of healthy relationships, with safe people we love, is mission critical for dealing with trauma.
- The truth about trauma is that it's impossible. Unbearable. Unbelievable.
- Faith has to grow in suffering. There are no easy answers, no firm way forward, no instant outcomes.
- Great gain means great loss.

TELL THE *Truth*

- What have you struggled to name? Is there a trusted friend who offers you safe space to share, so you can name it to tame it?
- Does pursuing perfection hinder you from pursuing wholeness?
- Consider making a timeline of your life. On a blank piece of paper, draw a horizontal line straight across the middle. Using points and lines, plot your highs above the line and your lows below it. How does it make you feel to think through the trauma and pain as you also celebrate the wins and joys?
- Who loves you without expectations and conditions? How does that make you feel? If you're struggling to think of someone, can you reflect on moments where

you felt loved by God or by a teacher, counselor, coach, social worker, or someone similar?

- How has your faith grown through suffering?
- What is your experience with the church? What is your hope for a community of faith where you can belong?

Part Two

TELL IT LIKE IT IS

five

THE TRUTH ABOUT ORDINARY

Transition, Grief, and Hope

> In the midst of chaos, there is also opportunity.
>
> Sun-Tzu, *The Art of War*

Trauma is not the only thing that produces change in our lives. The good stuff also has a ripple effect. Weddings, babies, graduations, relocations, and promotions all produce change in our daily life and relationships. Growing in our capacity to shift gears when life requires it keeps us alive to the moment and present in our pain so we can get beyond the past and focus on the future.

**In every transition,
there is a loss of control.**

When life begins to shift due to our own or someone else's choices, or because of a sudden loss, betrayal, or setback, we are thrust into the grey space, which feels like utter chaos. We experience a loss of identity or, at best, a changing identity, and we have to figure out how to live and survive in the unknown.

A time of uncertainty followed the death of Jesus: brutality in its highest form displayed itself at Golgotha, the temple curtain tore in two, the former religious order crumbled. But he didn't stay dead, and when Mary came to grieve at the tomb where they laid him, two angels appeared, saying, I think rather gleefully, "He's not here. He has risen." And she ran through the streets to tell the others something new was born. *Freedom.*

There was a time of mourning and then Jesus began to appear to people in their grief and distress, reminding them that he was alive and they, in turn, were alive in him—and renewal was born and would continue. A few of his disciples were utterly hopeless and broken, so they returned to what they knew best, since this whole "Jesus the Messiah, our rabbi" thing hadn't worked out. The men headed to sea and began to fish. They caught nothing until Jesus arrived on the scene and told them to cast the nets to the other side of the boat, something he had done the first time they met. Though skeptical once again, they agreed, and the nets began to tear from the weight of all the fish. As Peter recognized his Savior, he threw on his clothes, jumped in the water, and ferociously rushed to touch him, to hold him.

Later, Jesus appeared again to the disciples beside the Sea of Galilee. This is how it happened. Several of the disciples were there—Simon Peter, Thomas (nicknamed the Twin), Nathanael from Cana in Galilee, the sons of Zebedee, and two other disciples.

Simon Peter said, "I'm going fishing."

"We'll come, too," they all said. So they went out in the boat, but they caught nothing all night.

At dawn Jesus was standing on the beach, but the disciples couldn't see who he was. He called out, "Fellows, have you caught any fish?"

"No," they replied.

Then he said, "Throw out your net on the right-hand side of the boat, and you'll get some!" So they did, and they couldn't haul in the net because there were so many fish in it.

Then the disciple Jesus loved said to Peter, "It's the Lord!" When Simon Peter heard that it was the Lord, he put on his tunic (for he had stripped for work), jumped into the water, and headed to shore. The others stayed with the boat and pulled the loaded net to the shore, for they were only about a hundred yards from shore. (John 21:1–8)

And guess what Jesus was doing on the shore? Making a meal.

When they got there, they found breakfast waiting for them— fish cooking over a charcoal fire, and some bread.

"Bring some of the fish you've just caught," Jesus said. So Simon Peter went aboard and dragged the net to the shore. There were 153 large fish, and yet the net hadn't torn.

"Now come and have some breakfast!" Jesus said. None of the disciples dared to ask him, "Who are you?" They knew it was the Lord. Then Jesus served them the bread and the fish. This was the third time Jesus had appeared to his disciples since he had been raised from the dead. (vv. 9–14)

He didn't scold them for returning to their familiar work after being faced with his death, the loss of their rabbi, Jesus, and what would have felt like their entire mission and purpose. He didn't embarrass the disciples by asking them why they weren't fishing for men instead of fish. He didn't ask them why they hadn't begun seeking the renewal of the city, or tell them "I told you this would happen, now get back to work." Jesus, as a loving friend, advocate, and shepherd, provided the fish and even told them to bring him a few to fry. He invited them to sit in their pain, in his presence, and he began again to remind them who he was to them and who they were in the world.

The table is a place for remembrance.

Through the power of his presence, over a meal he's made, it feels as though he's calling them to remembrance, back to their final encounter before the cross. They were seated together at the table, where they took communion, ate and drank in sacred space, and listened as Jesus told them the truth about what it would take to live together in community after his death. The table was a safe place for the disciples, a place they regularly met with Jesus, a respite from the expectations and anxiety of the world pressing on them. Consistent time to dine where they could converse and connect, debate and transform.

In asking them to sit and eat, it's almost as if Jesus was reinstilling this sacred, ordinary practice of communion and fellowship. *Remember what I've shown you, that no one is disqualified. When it all goes down, come back to the table. Now go and make disciples, baptizing them in the name of the Father, the Son, and the Holy Spirit, and teaching them everything I have taught you. And don't forget I am with you, even to the end of the age.*

And to Peter, his beloved disciple, who didn't have the courage or strength to hold up under the political pressure and denied Jesus three times on the eve of his crucifixion, he offered an opportunity for redemption and public restoration of his ministry calling through a different question asked three times.

> After breakfast Jesus asked Simon Peter, "Simon son of John, do you love me more than these?"
>
> "Yes, Lord," Peter replied, "you know I love you."
>
> "Then feed my lambs," Jesus told him.
>
> Jesus repeated the question: "Simon son of John, do you love me?"
>
> "Yes, Lord," Peter said, "you know I love you."
>
> "Then take care of my sheep," Jesus said.
>
> A third time he asked him, "Simon son of John, do you love me?"
>
> Peter was hurt that Jesus asked the question a third time. He said, "Lord, you know everything. You know that I love you."
>
> Jesus said, "Then feed my sheep.
>
> "I tell you the truth, when you were young, you were able to do as you liked; you dressed yourself and went wherever you wanted to go. But when you are old, you will stretch out your hands, and others will dress you and take you where you don't want to go." Jesus said this to let him know by what kind of death he would glorify God. Then Jesus told him, "Follow me." (vv. 15–19)

Peter could have stepped off the boat and Jesus could have been like, "Hey! Brother, you sure didn't do right by me in the temple courts. Are you sure you love me?" Why didn't Jesus say that? Well, does public shaming work for you? If you experience a loss in relationship, does it help you to see someone for the first time in a while and have them immediately remind you of your failures with no intention of seeing your potential to change? Probably not, and more than likely your walls and defenses will go up before there is any chance for connection.

Jesus waited. He invited them to sit by the fire, cooked some fish, and maybe asked them how they were really doing after the traumatic experience of watching their Savior die an inhumane, uncivilized death. Maybe he told them how he conquered death and the grave, and perhaps they shed tears and laughed as they shared the sorrow of those silent days between the cross and resurrection.

We feed the people we love.

It's only after the meal, through their meaningful time together as a reminder of the relationship they really have, that Jesus turned to Peter and asked, "Simon Peter, do you love me more than these?"

John 21 tells us that Jesus's third question to Peter hurt. Peter was grieved, which was a turning point of his repentance as he moved into freedom and away from fear. His initial response reads with enthusiasm: "Of course, Jesus! You know I love you!" And then, in his second response, he seemed to understand the weight of what Jesus was asking, the gift he was about to receive in this powerful exchange of grace for shame. I wonder if he began to remember the big promise he professed before the cross: to die for Christ and to never deny Jesus. And then came the truth that he was unable to fulfill that promise.

Peter responded the third time with grief and a different level of devotion than he'd expressed in his denial; he had a truly surrendered posture and a determination to follow Christ even unto death. After that response, Jesus told Peter how he would die; that he would, in fact, be martyred for his radical faith, and with that prophetic picture of the future, Peter understood that he would never deny his Savior again.

What I find so remarkable about this is that Jesus was working with a regular guy from the block who had a fishing business. Peter didn't have a church. He wasn't a lead pastor or a rabbi in a temple. He was just a guy who left it all to follow Jesus. Nothing special about him except his heart and instinct to *follow*. Can we have a moment of silence to take in the repercussions of the glorious call of Christ for ordinary people?

Because, for real, how many times a day do we feel ordinary? We're attending classes, dropping kids off at school, checking out in the grocery store, folding somebody's chonies, and sitting in countless meetings that most definitely could have been emails.

Regular folks. Who are we to do something great? Why in the world would we be chosen for the good stuff? That's for the chosen ones, the seminary graduates, the evangelical council at the White House, the pastors and preachers on YouTube.

> **But this is the exact mental framework that Jesus came to bust wide open.**

He took a jackhammer to that cement when he started picking everyone—rich, mean people (Zacchaeus), ordinary women (Martha, Priscilla, Lydia), women with a reputation (the Samaritan woman at the well, Mary Magdalene, the woman with the issue of blood, the woman caught in the act of adultery), mothers (Mary the mother of Jesus), those with governmental authority (the centurion and his servants), Pharisees and religious leaders (Jairus), the sick and the lame (blind Bartimaeus, the lepers), young people (children he healed and invited to be with him).

That's because the kingdom of heaven is for whosoever will.

Who will follow? Who will trust God and take him at his Word? Because that is what settles it. You're the one the kingdom rests upon. You've been purposed to carry it forward. You, sister. You're it, and there's no priest, or pastor, or rabbi, or any other authority standing between you and God. You have been commissioned and called into the great work of heaven, feeding and teaching people in the Savior's love.

Your ordinary means everything to God. His hand of favor and blessing rests on you every moment of every day. There's no extraordinary "one day when." The seemingly insignificant moment is right in front of us, begging us to pay attention.

*Don't discount the small things just because
the world around you acts like they don't matter.
They do. And your strength is in them.*

Every simple act of love and kindness you do is what continues to restore and redeem this world. The coffee you pick up for a coworker. The handwritten note you mail to a mentor. The meal you make for the people you love. The household chores you complete with love and without complaining. The bills you pay that build your home. The smile you share with a stranger.

The yard you mow for a neighbor. The welcome basket you make for a new mother.

The ordinary moments of love and service that display our gratitude and character also put the kingdom of heaven on display so that people will see our lives and search for our Father. They will look at this great God we sacrifice everything for, because he is so good, and so loving, and so willing, and so able, and so worthy.

I've realized that's really how simple it is with God. The Savior of humankind came down to earth to give his life as a ransom for many, and he came to serve, not to be served. It's hard to fathom, isn't it? A king who comes to serve? Who does that? No king I know! And in the American church it can feel difficult to find a Christian with an important title who isn't pushing their agenda, candidate, brand, or event. It's hard to find spiritual leadership trustworthy enough to build the ordinary—people who are focused more on their integrity and other people than their image and platform.

And listen, I'm sorry about that. It grieves me and keeps me up at night. The awareness of my own capacity and potential to do this is with me always. We must each seek God daily to remain humble enough to resist pride and greed and to see the image of God in every person we meet so that we are available to serve.

> *Jesus can do anything with a person*
> *who is like him, a servant to any and all.*

At the beginning of the book of Acts, true to his mysterious nature, Jesus ascended, which literally means he floated right up to heaven. (Don't you just wish the *National Enquirer* had been in ancient Israel?) Then on the day of Pentecost, when the Lord sent his Spirit like he said he would, Peter, having been restored to his calling with the assurance from Christ, preached a bold, life-altering, earth-shaking word.

With the crowd listening, Peter tells it like it is, preaching the whole message of Jesus's life, death, and resurrection. He basically told them, *You did this! You killed Jesus!* (How good is this?!) He then followed with the good news of grace, and more than three thousand people decided on the spot to follow Jesus. Then the most radical scenario happened to these believers of Christ: the Holy Spirit fell on them, filling them all with the incarnate presence of Jesus, a literal, unimaginable, unbelievable miracle.

Their inherited experience with faith in God came through the stories of the Old Testament, where encounters with God, words of wisdom, and healing were possible only through a rabbi, prophet, or priest. Then Jesus came and was with them in the flesh, breaking open their belief systems, disrupting the world as they knew it, declaring his place as Messiah.

Because God is just and he is holy, a price needed to be paid for sin. He paid it by sending his Son to die on the cross for us so that we could live in unbroken fellowship with God by faith in Jesus Christ.

In Christ's death and resurrection, he gave us the Holy Spirit as a deposit on a guarantee of our future inheritance. Ephesians 1:14 in the Passion Translation says it like this: "He is given to us like an engagement ring is given to a bride, as the first installment of what's coming! He is our hope-promise of a future inheritance which seals us until we have all of redemption's promises and experience complete freedom—all for the supreme glory and honor of God!"

The Holy Spirit is our advocate and guide, and when the early believers were filled with the indwelling of God, through their faith in Christ, a life-giving community came alive. In the midst of their differences (which were many), God miraculously broke down barriers; they were speaking in other languages but could understand each other. In fact, people watching their joy and communication accused them of being drunk.

Then another miracle was spoken as Peter quoted the fulfillment of the prophet Joel's words, recorded almost nine hundred years before Christ:

> In the last days, God says,
> I will pour out my Spirit on all people.
> Your sons and daughters will prophesy,
> your young men will see visions,
> your old men will dream dreams.
> Even on my servants, both men and women,
> I will pour out my Spirit in those days,
> and they will prophesy. (Acts 2:17–18 NIV)

And don't we need that comfort today
in our youth-obsessed, gender-confused world?
We don't age out of the kingdom
of God. Women are not excluded.

The Lord will pour out his Spirit on all of his servants, and when the empowerment of God comes, in Christ, by the Holy Spirit—watch out, world, because no matter who you are or where you're from, no matter what you did last night or what has been done to you, choosing to follow Jesus means freedom from any cultural, ethnic, or economic barriers to pursuing purpose. Plus, you're *in*, and it's never too late for you. Again, we don't age out of the kingdom.

With this realization and powerful commissioning at Pentecost, the church of Jesus Christ is born. At this point, five thousand people are believers in Christ, and they start going out and doing good. The church is lit like a Christmas tree! People are getting radically healed, delivered, and saved, and just like when Jesus was with them, more and more men and women are moved with compassion, convicted of sin, and make decisions to follow and live in the way of Jesus. They're also getting accused, arrested, beaten, stoned, and tormented, but the unadulterated, provocative message of Christ compels them to do whatever is necessary to be transformed, to tell their story, to speak truth, to live a life that matters.

One of my favorite stories in the Bible happens right after this in Acts 3 and 4, when Peter and John were walking to the temple and a beggar asked them for money. And Peter, who had given up his business and probably wasn't packin' no cheddar, looked at the man, and said, "Silver or gold I do not have, but what I do have I give you. In the name of Jesus Christ of Nazareth, walk" (Acts 3:6). Then,

> Taking him by the right hand, he helped him up, and instantly the man's feet and ankles became strong. He jumped to his feet and began to walk. Then he went with them into the temple courts, walking and jumping, and praising God. When all the people saw him walking and praising God, they recognized him as the same man who used to sit begging at the temple gate called Beautiful, and they were filled with wonder and amazement at what had happened to him. (vv. 7–10 NIV)

The man who had been unable to walk for who knows how long stood up! And started walking! Can you believe this? He was literally paralyzed and, at a word, got up! This is how you know the Bible is still worth reading. Get a version that speaks to you, honey, because this is better than a dystopian novel series. *The Hunger Games* ain't got nothing on the book of Acts!

Of course, the next thing that happened is that the religious leaders were foaming-at-the-mouth mad, because if Jesus could heal everyone and anyone, and he could do it through his disciples, then the entire religious structure as they knew it was in danger of disruption. They didn't want to go through the loss and grief that accompanies transformation. The truth is, they rather liked the hierarchy. As long as there was someone beneath them—even if those folks were crippled, oppressed, or forgotten—then that meant they were still on top of the pyramid with the most power and privilege, which is exactly how they wanted it. As abolitionist Frederick Douglass said, "Power concedes nothing without a demand."*

The gospel of Jesus Christ demands that societal structures shift.

With their knickers in a twist, the religious leaders arrested Peter and John and dragged them into the temple court. I am laughing out loud as I write this, because can you imagine being dragged to court for *healing someone from paralysis?!* Why is religion so weird? The more bound we are within the

---

*Frederick Douglass, "West India Emancipation: Speech Delivered at Canandaigua, New York, August 4, 1857," *The Life and Writings of Frederick Douglass*, vol. 2, edited by Philip S. Foner (New York: International Publishers, 1950), 437.

establishment, the more the rulers celebrate, and the more freedom we find, the more the rulers want control. Have you noticed that?

If we change in order to pursue a better world for ourselves and for others, not everyone will celebrate that. Not everyone will sit down over a meal with us and give us a thumbs-up on our transformation and recovery. A friend or family member who stands to lose control if we get whole might ask, "Who in the world do you think you are?" A spiritual leader might tell us that miracles don't still happen, that we should just do what everyone else does, that the rules are there for us to obey them, that silence is better than truth telling. A coworker who has long benefited from our crippling insecurities and paralyzing fears might resist our newfound confidence, shutting us down in meetings and undermining our ideas.

Listen, in nearly every instance of chaos or change, some people will not budge an inch. They will hold on to what's familiar for dear life, fiercely guarding their sense of personal and systemic control and doing whatever they can to hinder others' embrace of something new.

This is why I love Peter and John. When faced with incarceration, murderous rage, and public humiliation, they chose to stand up, speak out, and live out their faith with an insane amount of grit and gumption.

To paraphrase, the disciples responded in the temple court with power: "Y'all are full of unbelief. Jesus, the one you killed, is the Messiah. He is the truth, and when it comes to not preaching in his name or speaking about him—yeah, that's gonna be a no for us, dog."

And the response from the religious world order gets me every single time: "When they saw the courage of Peter and

John and realized that they were unschooled, ordinary men, they were astonished and they took note that these men had been with Jesus" (4:13 NIV).

Unschooled, ordinary men
who had been with Jesus.

Peter and John were people just like us. They had been going about their daily life—fishing, parenting, learning, caretaking, homebuilding—until Jesus came along to say, *I see you. Come and follow me.* The men and women of Jesus's day experienced what was possible, a picture of the future that brought heaven down to earth with power and grace, transforming anyone and everyone willing to follow. And just like those early believers, in the following we become so immersed in Jesus's presence, in his love for others, in his compassionate plea to humanity through our lives that people can obviously tell we have been with him.

That's all we really need.
To be with Jesus.

We don't need credentials to follow our name—but if you do have those, sister, we are so proud of you. Yes to seminary degrees, master's degrees, and doctorates, but if you are working at the grocery store, local McDonald's, school, or hospital, or if you're reading this in a jail cell or a homeless shelter, you are just as qualified to be with Christ and spread his peace and healing power around like it's your full-time job.

And, thank God, we don't need to have our lives together to be qualified, because I never have and likely never will, but if you do, good for you! We don't need to have a lot of money, or all of the things we've prayed for, but if you do, fabulous! The favor of God is not dependent on our economic status. When Jesus stood in the temple and repeated the prophet Isaiah's words in Luke 4, he said, "The Spirit of the Lord is on me, because he has anointed me to proclaim good news to the poor. He has sent me to proclaim freedom for the prisoners and recovery of sight for the blind, to set the oppressed free, to proclaim the year of the Lord's favor" (vv. 18–19 NIV). Money does not indicate who God loves or how he loves us. It does not make us special; God does, and Jesus stood to declare that whatever we have or don't have, *now* is the time for good news for the poor, deliverance, recovery, release, and favor. It's not just for the rich and famous; it's for you and me as well. We also don't have to be completely healed, understand the chaos around us, or resist grieving our loss.

**All we need to do is follow him, be with him
in our ordinary, day-to-day life.**

We've got nothing to prove; we are at rest in his power and grace, and that, my friend, is a load off. Romans 12:1–2 from *The Message* version of the Bible says it like this:

So here's what I want you to do, God helping you: Take your everyday, ordinary life—your sleeping, eating, going-to-work, and walking-around life—and place it before God as an offering. Embracing what God does for you is the best thing you can do for him. Don't become so well-adjusted to your culture that you fit into it without even thinking. Instead, fix your attention on God. You'll be changed from the inside out. Readily recognize what he wants from you, and quickly respond to it.

Unlike the culture around you, always dragging you down to its level of immaturity, God brings the best out of you, develops well-formed maturity in you.

Sometimes, on the heels of great transition, we survey the rubble of devastation, of our loss, and it's easy to feel helpless or even hopeless. The tension in the transition from what was to what will be can be crushing. The first step in remembering hope is returning to ordinary, small things, because in chaos there is opportunity. We do what we know to do and trust God to meet us in the middle of it all. And I do want to tell you that, most of the time, trusting God and carrying on with the daily, small decisions of life don't result in some big rescue or removal from the situation we don't want to be in, but God will help us see his grace and goodness and see ourselves and others through the lens of hope.

In our ordinary moments, we can begin identifying times in the canker sore of chaos for us to be a truth teller, a healer, a lover of humanity. To spread peace and grace, kindness, and truth. To believe that the ancient words of the prophet Isaiah (Isa. 61:1–4), which Jesus quoted as his first message in the temple, saying, "Today this scripture is fulfilled in your hearing" (Luke 4:21 NIV), are still for us today.

We might not have everything, but in Christ, no matter the hell around us, we have good news to hear and proclaim. Our broken hearts are healed; we are set free; we have his favor. We receive beauty for our ashes, joy for our mourning, praise instead of our despair. We have purpose. We can rebuild, repair, and renew our lives and our communities; break free from the generational mindsets and history we may have been born into; and recognize the opportunity we have to change, to grow, and to care for and promote the marginalized in our midst—right in the middle of our chaos.

We are neither helpless nor hopeless. We are the helpers, the truth tellers, the healers, and the bridge builders. We can't do everything, but we can do the next thing, whatever it is, in front of us right now. Faithful in the small things. One step at a time. One day at a time.

Make a meal. Bake cookies for a neighbor. Buy groceries for a family. Look every person who serves you in the eye. Introduce yourself to someone. Speak up in that meeting. Tell your mom you love her. Call your friend. Hug a person who needs it. Serve at a local nonprofit. Host a book club in your home. Run a marathon. Take a Pilates class. Buy some shoes. Call your senators. Go on a pilgrimage. Sing a song. Write the next chapter. Pitch that pilot. Ask good questions over dinner. Share your greatest fear.

I don't know what's next for you, but I do know that you are well able to carry it out; so rise and get after it, my friend, with grace and gusto.

RISE, *Truth* TELLER

- In every transition there is a loss of control, so set the table for meaningful connection with loved ones and let it be a moment for remembrance.
- Don't discount the small things just because the world around you acts like they don't matter. They do. And your strength is in them.

- Jesus can do anything with a person who is like him, a servant to any and all. What we need to do is follow him and be with him in our ordinary, day-to-day life.
- We don't age out of the kingdom of God. Women are not excluded.
- The gospel of Jesus Christ demands that societal structures shift.
- We are neither helpless nor hopeless. We are the helpers, the truth tellers, the healers, and the bridge builders.

TELL THE *Truth*

- Are you currently going through a transition? What feels like a loss? What gives you hope?
- What do you think about the level of care Jesus provides when he is on the shore making a meal for his disciples after his resurrection?
- How have you felt cared for through a big change by God and by the people in your life?
- Do you know what it feels like to be excluded from the work of Christ or the church? How did you feel when you read that we don't age out of the kingdom, that you are included?
- *You're the one the kingdom rests upon. You've been purposed to carry it forward. You, sister. You have been commissioned and called into the great work of heaven, feeding and teaching people in the Savior's love.* What do you think of this audacious statement about you?

six

THE TRUTH ABOUT MARGIN

Here's All My Leftovers. You're Welcome.

Are you giving your family your emotional scraps?

blessed accountability question

Speaking of ordinary, my husband and I had our first married fight by the dishwasher. I'd been working late every night at my church job during the holiday season and I was on my final project, Christmas for Families. We worked with single parents and families experiencing a difficult financial season to cover needs and provide presents for Christmas morning. After I'd pulled my fourth or fifth all-nighter in a row, my husband, bless him, finally said no. Absolutely not. That's enough.

Margin, or lack thereof,
is a problem, though—you feel me?

"But, babe, these kids are not going to have Christmas!" I spewed at him, once again using a good thing I was responsible for in the community as an excuse to neglect the most important person I was responsible to in my home.

After shouting this, I then crawled into my internal process cave and, sitting alone like a totally exhausted, selfish jerk, I realized how wrong I was. My thoughts went a little like this: *What good is it to serve the entire community and not serve my spouse? How can people in the church feel my presence while the people I love have to take a number? Why am I working so hard to give my best to those I don't really even know (but want to please, help, or receive encouragement from) and give my brain-dead leftovers to my family?*

But this was also me: *Why can't my husband just understand how everyone needs me? Look at all the good I am doing! Why can't he let this slide? Why can't all my friends and family whom I haven't seen for months do the same? This is for the greater good! I am sacrificing myself. Can't they sacrifice for me?*

Cry me a literal river. I needed to say sorry. And I needed to flip my energy output on its head. I was giving my best to people I met in the streets, to partners I was working alongside in the community, to the pastoral team I worked with, to the volunteers I was leading—and my husband got all my leftovers. So did the rest of my family. And my friends. You know, all the people who will actually show up for me when I need them.

Transition means we must enlarge our capacity for more, but maybe not the more we initially think.

Margin is about capacity, and we cannot do it all, despite the women-shaming rhetoric out there that tells us to be all things to all people. We must set our priorities and focus so that we create a life we love and will continue to love years from now. We don't have to kill ourselves for anyone, not a voice in our head from the past, a boss or spiritual leader, a friend, or a family member. Sometimes doing less takes more of our mental energy because we literally don't even know how to stop ourselves from doing all the things we feel obligated to do. Even in loss, when our world feels like it's shrinking, our emotional and spiritual threshold still has to grow in order for us to recover. It's challenging to retrain our brains to think differently about our physical and emotional labor, but if we are going to do what we were created to do, it's necessary to reevaluate our roles and responsibilities in order to live freely and lightly.

I'll tell you what no one prepared me for in all those doggone premarital classes and mentor sessions: the transition from being a high-capacity female getting it *done* (who also crashed at home at 8:00 p.m. every night, sometimes with no dinner) to a wife working to build a life of vulnerability and intimacy with another person (which takes time, attention, and energy). Apparently, coming home from work with little more to give than a zombie and not having any more words left to speak was not going to build a marriage.

This was also the season I learned that chips and salsa with a bowl full of mixed greens was not a meal but an appetizer. My grocery budget went from $50 to $200 a week, and I was like, *What is happening right now? Who is eating all of this beef? Why is the salad rotting in the bottom drawer week after week? Who is going to cook all this stuff I just bought? Why do I already need to go to the store again? Why?*

The thing is, my husband had a huge job as well, but the man had his priorities in order. He had nothing to prove and he was not about to lose his family to ministry or work. He was not about that life. Thank God. Because the church had become my family, in a way, and while I regret nothing about giving my best, I regret that I stopped asking questions, stopped evaluating my role and the effect the work was having on my heart and my soul, and stopped allowing myself to connect with my deeper needs and desires. I didn't understand the internal motivations of my efforts, and the truth is I was scared to thoughtfully examine them. Building a life with Cody forced me, in the best way, to do so.

During our dating relationship, I was careful to risk my heart, releasing one day at a time, sharing fears and concerns as we built trust together. The pain of "too much, too soon" in previous relationships had given me costly wisdom, and I really didn't want to repeat the same mistakes. Have you done that before? Given yourself completely to a stranger, to "love at first sight" (more like lust at first sight)? Have you ever shared everything there is to share in less than six weeks and felt certain that he or she "Just gets me," "Really loves me for me," or "Makes me feel like no one ever has"?

Whew chile, y'all don't even know each other!

Has this person seen you at your worst? Will they show up for you at 3:00 a.m. when it all hits the fan? Do they know about your quirks and character flaws? Do you know about theirs? Do you even like each other outside of the attraction, the chemistry, and the desire to be loved? How do you know he isn't a serial killer? A pathological liar? A lowdown dirty rotten scoundrel? What if she's a workaholic, alcoholic, OCD psychopath? YOU DO NOT KNOW THIS PERSON.

Listen, I'm about to tell you a story to let you know that I know exactly what I am talking about. I know what it's like to compromise convictions, try to please an unpleasable person, and drown my dreams in an unreliable relationship. Once upon a time there was no margin in my life to meet a man like Cody, because I was messing around, wasting time with clowns.

I met this one dude in church after not dating for four years—yeah, that's right, I said four—and he turned out to be a complete pain in the behind. I gave him too much of my life, and I compromised too much of myself to make him happy. Of course, bullheaded as I can be sometimes, I blew right through the warning signs and red flags. Maybe it was partly because of the dating drought, the stress in my work life that so desperately needed a release, or the fact that I was still healing from my insecurities and learning to stand in my convictions in a relationship.

My "no is a complete sentence" still needed some practice.

I really don't know why I settled for this dude, except that I most definitely confused giving him grace with failing to hold him accountable for who he actually was and not who he said he was. While we were dating, the Acura 2.5TL I loved with a passion died and I had to get a new car, which my mom generously helped me buy. Without her, I would have been biking all over Los Angeles, I guess, because that's all I could afford at the time on my pathetic assistant's salary. (You know, the kind where you work ten- to twelve-hour days but can barely afford to put gas in your car? Yeah, that kind of pay.)

I bought a Volkswagen Passat, and just like I picked men at the time, I picked a car that looked good but wasn't worth the hassle and definitely wasn't going the distance with me. Charcoal grey, tinted windows, great sound system, shiny rims, seat warmers. (Who invented these? Give them the Nobel Peace Prize!) She was a beauty.

Internally, though, that fly-looking car had a sludgy engine, had been recalled a few times, and had an oil pan right under the front of the car that was covered only by a plastic plate, so when I went over a pothole or speed bump a little too fast, she'd bust, and oil would flow like a river runs through it. Except Brad Pitt or whoever else was in that movie was not there to help—or pay for it. She was a lemon, and nobody would let me give her—and her ridiculous, high-interest monthly payments—back. I was not even making enough money to cover the payments, and there were many months my mom had to help me pay it, because these are the dumb things you do when you are twenty-four and think you're going to get fired if you don't have a car for your slave job and are too proud to work at the grocery store (where the pay was likely better).

Due to my pitiful salary, I also had a part-time job as a personal trainer in the evenings. One eventful evening, I was pulling double duty. I'd arrived at work at 8:30 a.m., and at the end of my day I needed to drive one of the kids to a youth event an hour away. This event would last a few hours, so I planned, per usual, to train a client in the city while waiting for the event to end. My client lived in a beautiful building with valet parking, and when I went to go get the car after our session, I saw the puddle of oil all around the car. My eyes filled with tears, and my heart raged with fear. I knew my bosses would kill me if they had to drive the hour and back to get their daughter from the youth event, and I also knew I didn't have the money to fix this again.

Let me put this riveting story on pause to say thank you to the famous money advisors with radio shows for all of your helpful advice. Has anyone ever noticed that these books and resources are really for rich people who don't know how to manage their money and not for people who are actually poor? Like, what am I supposed to save when I live below the poverty line? How can I pay myself first when I can't even pay my rent? What'chu talkin' 'bout, Willis? How can I get a third job when I already work ten to twelve hours a day, plus my time spent as a personal trainer? Does anyone else struggle to receive some of the wisdom from financial resources written from the perspective of, "Hey, we've got a lot to manage, and a lot of help with our kids, and we live in the 'burbs, and we just need to stop eating out and drinking Starbucks and we'll save for retirement"? Mmmm-kay.

Anyway, I was still figuring out how to ask for help, but I had been dating this dude, aka Team No Boundaries, for nearly a year, so I figured I could call him and see if he could help me. This fool had two cars and a massive salary, and beside the fact that he often asked me to pay for our meals because he thought we should share the "burden" (just run, okay, if this is you right now: *run*), he also did not like coming through in a clutch. He really didn't like to be bothered with any problems, even though he was giving me plenty.

He answered the phone. I kid you not, it was 8:00 p.m., and when I asked him for help, he let out the biggest, most annoyed *ugh* and then said, "Come on, Ashley, you know I have to get up early!" Mind you, I was not even ten minutes from his apartment, and I was beside myself with anger. What in the world was I doing with this dude? Before I was a Christian, I would have dropped him like a bad habit. Why, in the name of all things sacred and holy, had I been okay with this?

That moment was a gift to me. He whined like he needed some cheese and then finally decided to come and get me. While I waited with the tow truck and the valet guys—who were taking great care of me—I pictured myself in a minivan (which is another sign that he was not the one, if our future included a minivan) with kids in the back, calling their father, and him grumbling about having to help. *Nope, that's it. All done.* I would not want my sons to be like him, and I would not want my daughters to think this is what a man does.

He took me back to his place, mopey and silent the entire way, and I took his second car to pick up the teen at the event and drive her home. As I prayed and cried myself to sleep, I asked God to help me. I had come so far in my recovery journey, and I couldn't allow one relationship to set me back. This was not the life I wanted. I felt encouraged to fast from the relationship. No texts, calls, emails, or hangouts, just a full three-week break. During that time I was housesitting for a friend, and on my knees in her living room with Coldplay's "Fix You" on repeat, I asked God to show me the truth. No matter how bad it would hurt, I wanted to see what I had chosen, what I had settled for, and why I had compromised.

I began to see the last year with Mr. Cheapskate, and as I looked with a perspective unencumbered by his presence and his control, the presence of God showed me my deeply rooted belief that I didn't deserve anything better. That belief housed many lies, such as there are no faithful men out there anyway; I would always need to be a woman at work, even in my home and marriage; I would never experience rest or release from pressure and pleasing; that it was my job to keep a man happy and satisfied; that God expected me to give people grace, even to my own detriment.

He also showed me how afraid I was of true intimacy, of real connection and vulnerability, and that I didn't fully trust that God is good to me and would do good for me. Two things came out of that three-week fast: I quit the boyfriend, who, by the way, went on a cruise with his boys during the fast and came bragging to me afterward with, "I had so many opportunities to cheat on you, and I didn't. I could have, but I didn't." What do you want—you no-self-control, stingy, selfish leech—a parade for doing what you are supposed to do? BOY, BYE.

And I quit my job.

I felt God asking me to make room for more.

There was no tangible evidence that he would come through for me, but I felt that making the leap would be the best thing I could do for myself. I chose to trust him. Isaiah 54 was the promise God gave me:

> "Sing, barren woman,
>   you who never bore a child;
> burst into song, shout for joy,
>   you who were never in labor;
> because more are the children of the desolate woman
>   than of her who has a husband,"
>   says the LORD.
> "Enlarge the place of your tent,
>   stretch your tent curtains wide,
>   do not hold back;
> lengthen your cords,
>   strengthen your stakes.
> For you will spread out to the right and to the left;
>   your descendants will dispossess nations
>   and settle in their desolate cities.
> "Do not be afraid; you will not be put to shame.
>   Do not fear disgrace; you will not be humiliated.

You will forget the shame of your youth
  and remember no more the reproach of your
    widowhood.
For your Maker is your husband—
  the LORD Almighty is his name—
the Holy One of Israel is your Redeemer;
  he is called the God of all the earth.
The LORD will call you back
  as if you were a wife deserted and distressed in
    spirit—
a wife who married young,
  only to be rejected," says your God.
"For a brief moment I abandoned you,
  but with deep compassion I will bring you back.
In a surge of anger
  I hid my face from you for a moment,
but with everlasting kindness
  I will have compassion on you,"
    says the LORD your Redeemer. (vv. 1–8 NIV)

*Rejected and desolate, barren and disgraced,
fearful and humiliated, I was reminded by the Lord
that I would not be put to shame, that he had compassion
on me, that he was my Maker and my Redeemer,
and he asked me to enlarge, stretch, lengthen,
and strengthen.*

In order to make room, I had to reorder my margin, letting go of what could kill me to embrace what would build me.

It was hard and messy, and I made mistakes, but I did leave two of the most suffocating situations in my life, spaces that left me feeling undervalued, unappreciated, and frankly, like "the help," as if my entire existence was to serve theirs. I realized in all that work, striving, people pleasing, and stress, my soul was shouting, *Somebody see me! The real me! Please!*

I had to take responsibility for what I was not saying, because an unspoken expectation is an unfair expectation. At the same time, I think deep down we all know when we are treating people dishonorably, and if we are not willing to change, we cannot expect people to continue to work with us. I am thankful that God, as the Ancient of Days, keeps an accurate account. He's got the receipts and will hold each of us accountable for what we have done. It felt scary to get out, to trust that God had something better for me, but I count that as one of the most defining moments of my life so far. I made room for what I really wanted, by faith, in spite of the fear I felt.

And it led me down a path of healing and deeper levels of recovery. Meeting Cody was an unexpected surprise, and his peaceful presence and generous love scared the snot out of me. I think part of the reason I was avoidant in our first year of marriage was my constant fear of real intimacy. Oh my word, how I wanted to be seen, and goodness gracious, did I struggle to fully experience that.

Communication was my biggest roadblock. Do you know what that's like? To long so desperately to share and connect, to put truth into words, and instead find yourself isolating, erecting barriers, keeping busy, acting fine, staying quiet? Whenever Cody and I needed to have a difficult conversation, I found myself shutting down, like there was a muzzle over my mouth, and no matter how hard I tried I couldn't shake the shame of silence in my life that had followed me since childhood. I didn't mean to be an emotional stonewaller in our marriage; it just happened that way, and I lacked the capacity to bridge the gap of my understanding as to why it was happening. Cody is a connector, relational to the core, and has a need to come together when things get intense. I am also highly relational but have a need to separate when things get intense.

I expected him to give up and be like, "What is wrong with you? Why can't you talk? What is your problem? Say what you mean!" Instead, he would stay with me, keeping his presence close even though we weren't able to discuss anything. When he said, "Ashley, I know you're not ready to talk right now, but when you are, I'm here," it was like Tasha Cobbs entered our living room belting, "I hear the chains falling!" It felt like warm liquid poured down my aching throat, into my anxious gut, and love started to replace fear. And for the first time with a man, I found that breaking the silence was possible.

Shame doesn't compound shame when love is the response.

Cody taught me that God doesn't remove his presence when we struggle. In what feels like heaven, or hell, he stays with us, holds us, and loves us all the way to wholeness and integrity.

> Where can I go from Your Spirit?
> Or where can I flee from Your presence?
> If I ascend into heaven, You are there;
> If I make my bed in hell, behold, You are there.
> If I take the wings of the morning,
> And dwell in the uttermost parts of the sea,

Even there Your hand shall lead me,
And Your right hand shall hold me.
If I say, "Surely the darkness shall fall on me,"
Even the night shall be light about me;
Indeed, the darkness shall not hide from You,
But the night shines as the day;
The darkness and the light are both alike to You.
(Ps. 139:7–12 NKJV)

All that to say Cody and I came far in our first year in the areas of communication, honesty, and vulnerability. I learned from the dishwasher shenanigans that I personally still had a ways to go to remain connected consistently, and that we as a couple needed to learn to rest. We spent the next year flipping our energy output on its head. We wanted the best to flow in our home and to do our best in our other spheres of influence, but not at the expense of our personal intimacy with God and with each other.

Our first step was growing in accountability, and not the kind where you meet for coffee once a month and act like you know each other. We wanted to live together in deep, abiding relationship, where we were known and loved and could have the honor and responsibility of intimately knowing and loving others. Cody and I are huge fans of Dr. Jim Burns, founder of HomeWord, and his teaching on marriage, family, and parenting. He is an incredible advocate of accountability through deeply rooted friendships, and he has a list of twelve questions to ask friends in order to live present and remain honest about where we really are. Cody and I both decided to get in a group with a few trusted friends and start going through these questions every week.

1. Do you like the person you are becoming?

2. Is your heart for God shrinking or growing?

3. Are you giving your family only your emotional scraps?

4. Have you done anything that compromised your integrity with the opposite sex?

5. Have you compromised your integrity with finances?

6. Is your character submitted to Christ?

7. Are you faithfully involved with worship and service?

8. Is your pace of life sustainable?

9. Have you allowed a person or circumstance to rob you of joy?

10. Are you taking care of your body through physical exercise and proper eating and sleeping habits?

11. Have you been faithful to regular connections with Jesus?

12. Have you lied on any of your answers with me?*

How good is the last one? I laughed out loud the first time I read it.

In that first year of doing this with four other friends, questions two, three, eight, and eleven were my main areas of growth, especially number two. Addressing the other three helped me fix the fact that my answer was often yes. The pace of my life was unsustainable. My heart for God (in spite of the fact that I was working for a church) was shrinking, and because I felt like I worked for Jesus, I sure didn't want to spend

*Doug Fields, "12 Accountability Questions for Leaders," *HomeWord*, February 6, 2015, https://homeword.com/articles/12-accountability-questions -for-leaders/#.XJ5iHxNKjBl.

any time with him outside of work. *Bro, I just saw you, okay? You're making me tired.*

Our second step was to begin studying the Sabbath, because neither of us took one! After Cody learned that not taking a Sabbath was one of the two things you could be stoned for in the Old Testament (adultery is the other), we decided to get our lives together. I learned that Sabbath and shalom (peace) are always present together in Scripture; they go hand in hand. **Without Sabbath, there is no peace. And without peace, there is no justice.** I had always wondered why violating Sabbath made the list of the Ten Commandments, and it's also the closing thought of my favorite passage of Scripture, Isaiah 58, which didn't make sense to me either.

Through that study, I began to fully understand that we are human beings, not human doings, and when we don't take a Sabbath we begin to act like a machine rather than a person. What follows very quickly is that we begin to think of others as machines as well, and people who become machines to us are easy to exploit. Without a Sabbath, we live in a little microcosm we've created, and it's easy to think that the world won't work without us, that we are in control of everything, when the opposite is actually true. The world is expansive and large, rich and beautiful, and we couldn't possibly hold it all together—only God has the capacity to do that. The world works just fine without us, and our part, though extraordinary and significant, is small, to say the least.

Without a Sabbath, we begin to falsely believe that our thing is superior or inferior to another's, and it becomes easier to feel like we have some sort of ownership over people rather than a responsibility to them. We begin to shrink people down to what they can do for us, how they can build our thing, rather than allowing them to just be a person made in the image of God. Funny thing is, we can do this with our children, spouse, employees, and communities of faith, because it's a mindset, and the number of people we are influencing is irrelevant.

In his must-read book, *The Rest of God*, Mark Buchanan makes a very strong case for why we need to restore the Sabbath to our lives. In chapter 6, he lays out the two biblical accounts of the Ten Commandments, both of which include a Sabbath. He writes,

> Exodus grounds Sabbath in creation. Deuteronomy grounds it in liberation. Exodus remembers Eden, Deuteronomy Egypt. In Exodus, Sabbath-keeping is about imitating divine example and receiving divine blessing. In Deuteronomy, it is about taking hold of divine deliverance and observing divine command.
>
> Exodus looks up. Deuteronomy looks back. Exodus gives theological rationale for rest, and Deuteronomy historical justification for it. One evokes God's character, the other his redemption. One calls us to holy mimicry—be like God; the other to holy defiance—never be slaves again. One reminds us that we are God's children—the work of his hands, the other that we are no one's chattel, not Pharoah's, not Nebachadnezzar's, not Xerxes', not Beelzebub's.
>
> One is invitation. The other is warning.*

He goes on to use the story in Exodus of Pharaoh, who was a taskmaster, a slave driver who never let the people rest, to illustrate our tendency to work without ceasing, to struggle under a constant, internal whipping that drives us to a life

*Mark Buchanan, *The Rest of God: Restoring Your Soul by Restoring Sabbath* (Nashville: Thomas Nelson, 2006), 85–102.

without rest. In the story, free labor wasn't enough for this oppressive, evil leader. In fact, every time the Israelite slaves got used to their workload, Pharaoh would add more work while also removing resources necessary to accomplish the task in the unreasonable time frame he'd given. No matter what tasks were completed, it was never enough.

I realized that throughout my life, I have continued to choose situations, particularly at work and in dating, with this same mindset. I had a taskmaster in my head that I falsely believed was God, driving me to unrelenting efforts, to perform for approval, try to live up to an impossible personal standard, and do my best to please people who couldn't be pleased. With God's help, it was necessary for me to learn that I am created in God's image and therefore liberated to live at peace with myself, and others, through rest.

While I never, ever want to make light of the real experience and struggle of those who have experienced slave labor, I do want to make a point about living with this kind of taskmaster mentality.

It will kill you.

Without addressing the attitudes that drive us to resist rest, we cannot make the necessary changes we need to in order to enter a lifestyle of Sabbath. That's the first step. While there's no easy, overnight method that will suddenly change your life, I've put together a helpful how-to below that will either encourage or depress you. Maybe both.

1. Admit there's a problem. Acknowledge the taskmaster, if you have one, and serve them a notice. They are not God. You will no longer be under their thumb.

2. Start with small changes. Leave the office on time. Keep commitments to yourself. Schedule time to rest and don't cancel. Try the accountability questions with some folks you love who also love you.

3. Put your phone down. That thing is an anxiety-inducing heart attack waiting to happen. You are not a twenty-four-hour pharmacy. No one should have access to you every hour of every day.

4. Remove work email from your phone on your days off. I don't even know how to tell you how this changed my life. Nope, I am not even going to look, because I am off. Sorry if you aren't, but you are grown and we used to have to communicate through pagers and phones that hung on the wall, so I am sure you'll all be fine without me on the days you are not paying me to work.

5. Take a break from social media. At least once a week, just don't even look. If you missed anything juicy, your friends will likely send you a text, meme, screenshot, or GIF. Also, you won't be so angry at all the people who are on vacation while you are busy not having the budget to take one. (Maybe that's just me . . .)

6. Stop *shoulding* all over yourself. *I should respond. I should have taken care of that. I should do more than is required of me on every project, and treat absolutely everything as a top priority. I should be better at this, that, and the other thing.* No, you shouldn't, and even if you should, guilt and shame are not a permanent solution to change; they are an invitation to the crazy train, which you are currently trying to de-board.

7. Just don't respond. I am not talking about irresponsible, lazy correspondence. I am talking about eliminating the taskmaster who tells you that everything is urgent. No, it's not. Skip the notifications. Delete the email. Ignore the question. Read the text and don't text back if it's not necessary. Don't forget, less than twenty-five years ago, we couldn't even text!

8. Choose a Sabbath and keep it. A full twenty-four hours each week where you don't do anything that you have to do but only things that you choose to do. Share a meal with people you love. Take some time for yourself. Do the thing that makes you feel alive, even if it's just a bubble bath, a walk, or reading in your sweats. Yes, the first few weeks you will feel like the world is falling apart at the seams, like it just can't hold up without you. Sister, yes it will. You are not the glue of the universe.

9. If you have little children (or teens, I imagine but can't know for sure), there's no hope for you. Kidding—not kidding. No, you cannot sleep in on your Sabbath. No, you cannot just go to a movie, because it will cost you $150 for babysitting, tickets, and one pack of M&Ms. No, you cannot let them fend for themselves because you need a break. Just do your best. At nap time, don't do laundry. Go lay down, make a meal you can eat in peace, or watch *Law & Order SVU*. If you have a partner, take turns giving each other a break to do what you want, or ask a friend for a few hours of help. And put those jokers to bed at 7:00 p.m. on your days off so you can live your best life.

10. Give yourself time to catch a rhythm. It might take you a full year to find what works for you and your family. You may have to plot your exit from a job that's killing you. You might have to ask for a work-from-home day so you can pick the kids up once a week. You might realize that solitude is your sweet spot, or that you need more time with friends. Don't give up and keep trying.

Working under an internal slave driver will destroy you, and it's highly likely that if you're living under one, you'll find yourself in situations where all that inner toil is repeated in your external circumstances. Our efforts are never enough for others, because they are not enough for us, and we have to find a way to get alone with God and do business with him in order to accept his love and receive his grace to change. To help ourselves change, we make room for life-giving friendships and community where we are loved and understood, seen and heard, so we can rise to our full potential through accountability.

Then we must learn to rest so we can focus on using our energy effectively, to make the tough decisions to quit what needs to be quit, to make room for the right things. **Sabbath restores us to sanity.** In our rest, we gain perspective and get direction. We return to love, and when love leads us, our anxiety-driven thirst for more, more, more, is quenched, because God is enough. Letting that sink into our spirit leads to knowing we are enough. We can release ourselves from the pressure of the taskmaster to receive grace from our Savior and Redeemer. In this, we give up our desire to be God and persist with the fundamental understanding that God is good, that he does good, and he will be good to us.

Rest replaces anxiety. Love devours fear. Hope overshadows dread. Joy overcomes our sorrow. Make room for more.

RISE, *Truth* TELLER

- We need margin to think, to process, to make healthy choices, to heal and move forward.
- Transition means we must enlarge our capacity for more, but maybe not the *more* we initially think.
- In order to make room, we must take time to reorder our margin, letting go of what could kill us to embrace what will build us.
- Repeat after me: "No" is a complete sentence.
- God doesn't remove his presence when we struggle. He stays with us no matter what (Ps. 139).
- Accountability in the form of loving, genuine, authentic relationships keeps us aware of how we are living and is deeply connected to our convictions and values.
- Living under the taskmaster mentality, rather than the freedom of God's rest, will kill us.
- Sabbath restores us to sanity.

TELL THE *Truth*

- Take inventory of your calendar, including things like entertainment and social media. Where do you spend the bulk of your time?

- Do you lack the margin you need in your time, relationships, finances, or career? How does that impact you and your faith?

- Is there anything, or anyone, that you've been unwilling to give up, even though it's hurting you not to? Reflect for a minute—why do you think this is true for you?

- Do you struggle to say no? Why or why not?

- Who are your closest friends and family? Looking at the list of accountability questions, is there anything you would struggle to share with the people you love? Can you take a step deeper in relationship this week? (I highly recommend the book *Safe People* by Dr. Henry Cloud if you are struggling to find healthy people to trust.)

- Do you take a Sabbath? What would it take for you to trust God with a weekly rest?

seven

THE TRUTH ABOUT CHRISTIANS

Life at the Table

> When Jesus himself wanted to explain to his disciples what his forthcoming death was all about, he didn't give them a theory, he gave them a meal.
>
> N. T. Wright

When we are stripped of our comforts and our certainty, a meal is in order. I know what you might be thinking. How did the girl with the eating disorder come to value the table as a primary path to spiritual formation? I am not sure, to be honest, but like the blind man Jesus healed who was tried in court for his healing said, "*All I know* is that I once was blind, and now I see" (see John 9:25). And, as Joseph said in Genesis 50:20 to his brothers who had sold him into slavery, "You intended to harm me, but God intended it for good to accomplish what is now being done, the saving of many lives" (NIV). What the devil meant to destroy me, God has used, and is using, for my good.

So, once obsessed with food,
I became obsessed with family.

It's wonderful to me that we have a shared, human need: to eat in order to live. The way of Jesus, as we've already explored together, often included a meal. (Who else is thankful for this?) At the end of the Bible is the marriage supper of the Lamb, and since Adam and Eve kicked off humanity's fallen nature by eating fruit from the forbidden tree, it seems fitting that God would begin the final redemption of humankind with a meal. I like the table's vulnerability—although I know its pain as well, when control, silence, or shame shape the mind concerning the meal. Still, it's stunning what sharing a meal has the potential power to teach us. That the ground is level at the foot of the cross. That we are different and yet the same. That we are worth looking in the eye. That what we have to say matters. That listening to others is important. That our highest and best connection is not an email, text message, comment, or direct message.

It's face-to-face, together in our need. I like that.

We do family dinner once a week at our house, because all the other days we are doing our best with chicken nuggets and mac 'n cheese for the kids, and then Cody and I scarf down something together, usually in front of the tube, wide-eyed and comatose. But on Friday nights we clean our table that has served as a LEGO work space all week and place two taper candles in the middle of it. Levi, our oldest, loves to help me light them, and he gets very excited to sit and to serve.

"Mom, would you like some French fries?" "Dad, how about some ketchup?" "Lucas, do you need anything?" Our youngest grunts, claps, or shakes his head in response, and we get ourselves settled, passing food around, and then one of us prays to thank God for the meal and the moment.

We ask each other about our week, one thing we loved, and one thing that was difficult. We talk with no electronics to interrupt us, and we do our best to share honestly about what's happening in our lives.

Family dinner became important to us, in our large urban city context, because we wanted to have time set apart to talk, to begin our Sabbath, without the influence of our phones or *Paw Patrol*. We want our boys to understand how to connect and communicate, and how important it is to just put down the phone, which is kind of hard for us, to be honest. I think I'm pretty addicted to the thing. (My Instagram scrolling while I am peeing as evidence, Exhibit A, your honor.)

As we sit together, we are energized when we connect, speak our truth, and listen to each other process our emotions and our experiences for the week. At best, our tables serve as a pathway for relationship and a solution to loneliness and isolation. When we lack community and connection, when we are drowning alone, we're prone to begin hurting ourselves and others.

Throughout Scripture, we see the table as a place to sit with tension and conflict, to see wrongs made right, to experience healing and deliverance— to witness sheer, audacious heroism and spunk.

Meals are still meaningful,
even in our modern day.

Okay, so check it. . . . May I introduce you to Jael?

Her story starts with this awesome judge and prophet, Deborah, who was leading the entire nation of Israel. In Judges 4, she'd just about had it with Sisera, the commander of King Jabin's army, who had been oppressing Israel for twenty years. Deborah told her main general, Barak, that he should prepare to go and fight with ten thousand of his men, and he said, "Well, if you'll go with me, I'll go, but if you won't, then I'm not going." And she responded, "Fine, but because you decided to do this, God is going to hand the victory to a woman." He was like, *Story of my life*, and they went off to fight.

They took down the entire army, but Sisera managed to escape on foot and headed to the tent of Jael, wife of Heber the Kenite, with whom he had an alliance. She invited him in, and he was all, "I'm thirsty," and she said, "Cool, cool, here's some milk from my table," and he drank and fell fast asleep. Then, while he slept, she drove a tent peg through his temple into the ground, and he died.

About that time Barak showed up, all kinds of late, and must have thought, *Here's the woman Deb told me about*, because Jael said, "Come and I will show you the man you're looking for." And there he was, dead as a doornail with a tent peg in his head. Then the Israelites kept pressing until Jabin was destroyed too.

And that's all we know about Jael. We don't know her family dynamics, except that she was married to Heber the Kenite and there was peace between him and King Jabin. The Bible does not tell us if she went against her husband's wishes or if they both didn't like what was happening to the Israelites and no longer wanted to keep the alliance. We don't know where her husband was at the time, actually, or any details beyond what is written, and while you won't catch me advocating for war in general, this story gives me great hope for women who risk everything and do what needs to be done for the greater good. It's also amazing to see Jael partner with another powerful female, Deborah, to eliminate the very serious threat to her community.

Therefore, the table is a pathway for justice. And not just for Israel through the hands of Jael, but through another brave young woman, Esther.

I know Esther gets lifted up as the poster child of great opportunity and strength (and rightly so), but if we don't romanticize the story, we see an orphaned Jewish teenager who lived with her cousin Mordecai. He worked for the king of Persia, Xerxes, and had been taken from Jerusalem to Babylon and was living in Persia. Xerxes's wife, Queen Vashti, refused to come and parade her beauty during a festival, and the king, under the advice of the usual goons on a power trip, decided Vashti would be banned from his presence and that another woman, more specifically a virgin, would take her place as queen.

His men went out into all 126 provinces and selected the best young virgins they could find, Esther being one of them, and brought them all into the king's harem. Yes, I said harem. For one year, they received beauty treatments before their one shot before the king, and long story short, Esther was the one he picked. Scholars estimate she was about fifteen years old, and Xerxes was about forty. (Ew.)

Nevertheless, Esther persisted and was given an opportunity to save her people when Haman, who was as racist as a person can be, realized her cousin Mordecai was a Jew, all because he wouldn't bow down to Haman. A shady man obsessed with power, Haman gets the king to issue an edict calling for all the Jews to be destroyed. As the new executive order gets posted all over the land, the Jews begin to fast and pray.

Mordecai visited Esther to tell her, "Listen, you have to do something," but she was like, "*You* listen, you know if I go visit the king unsummoned he could kill me, so how about no, Mordecai." But then he said something along the lines of, "Don't think because you're queen now that he won't kill you too. And who knows but that you have come to your royal position for such a time as this?" And Esther said, "You're right. Tell everybody to keep fasting and praying, and I will go. If I perish, I perish."

She went before the king and he didn't kill her; in fact, he welcomed her and asked her what she wanted, even up to half his kingdom. And she said, "Please, you and Haman come to dinner tonight." So, they did. And at dinner, the king asked her the same question, and she asked them to come to dinner again the following night. They agreed, and Haman left thinking he was the bee's knees and bragged to his wife and family, but he got in a sour mood when he saw Mordecai because he was a racist bigot on a power trip. Haman's family gave him terrible advice, because birds of a feather flock together, and he came up with an elaborate way to kill Mordecai by impaling him on a seventy-five-foot pole in public, and this crazy man actually built the pole in preparation.

That same night, Xerxes couldn't sleep, because God is good, and the king realized that Mordecai had stopped an assassination attempt on his life. The next day, he saw Haman and asked, "What should be done for the man the king delights to honor?" You already know Haman was full of his little self, and he thought the king was talking about him, so he listed all the things he wanted. But he was really in for a rude awakening. The king said, "Ooh, good ideas! Go on and do all that for Mordecai."

Read it for yourself . . .

That night the king could not sleep; so he ordered the book of the chronicles, the record of his reign, to be brought in and read to him. It was found recorded there that Mordecai had exposed Bigthana and Teresh, two of the king's officers who guarded the doorway, who had conspired to assassinate King Xerxes.

"What honor and recognition has Mordecai received for this?" the king asked.

"Nothing has been done for him," his attendants answered.

The king said, "Who is in the court?" Now Haman had just entered the outer court of the palace to speak to the king about impaling Mordecai on the pole he had set up for him.

His attendants answered, "Haman is standing in the court."

"Bring him in," the king ordered.

When Haman entered, the king asked him, "What should be done for the man the king delights to honor?"

Now Haman thought to himself, "Who is there that the king would rather honor than me?" So he answered the king, "For the man the king delights to honor, have them bring a royal robe the king has worn and a horse the king has ridden, one with a royal crest placed on its head. Then let the robe and horse be entrusted to one of the king's most noble princes. Let them robe the man the king delights to honor, and lead him on the horse through the city streets, proclaiming before him, 'This is what is done for the man the king delights to honor!'"

"Go at once," the king commanded Haman. "Get the robe and the horse and do just as you have suggested for Mordecai the Jew, who sits at the king's gate. Do not neglect anything you have recommended."

So Haman got the robe and the horse. He robed Mordecai, and led him on horseback through the city streets, proclaiming before him, "This is what is done for the man the king delights to honor!"

Afterward Mordecai returned to the king's gate. But Haman rushed home, with his head covered in grief, and told Zeresh his wife and all his friends everything that had happened to him.

His advisers and his wife Zeresh said to him, "Since Mordecai, before whom your downfall has started, is of Jewish origin, you cannot stand against him—you will surely come to ruin!" While they were still talking with him, the king's eunuchs arrived and hurried Haman away to the banquet Esther had prepared. (Esther 6:1–14 NIV)

I know. I am laughing too. Haman cried to his advisers and his wife about how the plot had twisted, and instead of saying, "Hey, we gave you some really bad advice; you shouldn't have built that pole," they said, "Well, seems like your life is coming to ruins." #sad.

Haman then rushed off to dinner number two with the king and Esther. King Xerxes asked Esther again, "What do you want? I'll give it to you, even up to half the kingdom," and she pled the case for her people, who were in severe danger, and exposed Haman, who was sitting right there. Haman was now sweating bullets, and the king was so mad that the Bible says he left his wine and went to the palace garden.

While he was gone, Haman begged Queen Esther for his life, but unfortunately for him, as the king came back, from his angle it looked like Haman was not begging but rather molesting the queen. Then Xerxes was told by his eunuchs (likely the same ones who prepared Esther for him) that Haman had built that ginormous pole of death right by his house. The king was like, IMPALE HIM ON IT. And not only did that happen but Esther got Haman's estate and Mordecai got his signet ring. A new executive order (written by Mordecai) was issued and sealed with that ring. Jews were given the right to assemble and protect themselves, and the order for them to be destroyed was reversed.

Sister, won't the good Lord do it?

He lifted up a young Jewish woman from a marginalized people group, for such a time as this, and then he used her complex circumstances to combat a governmental order for genocide and bring freedom to that very group of people. Esther hit her knees, calling for the people to pray and fast. She acted in spite of her fear, risking her life and using what she had—favor with the king, a capacity to set a table, an ability to discern the right timing to expose her enemy—and God was on her side.

I think of Psalm 23, where the psalmist sings, "Yea, though I walk through the valley of the shadow of death, I will fear no evil; for you are with me; your rod and your staff, they comfort me. You prepare a table before me in the presence of my enemies; you anoint my head with oil; my cup runs over" (vv. 4–5 NKJV). And run over it did.

In the life of Esther, the table brought freedom. In addition to freedom, the table invites the miracle of life.

In 1 Kings, there's a story of a widow and her young son. A devastating famine hit the widow's land, and she planned to make a final meal with the little flour and oil she had left and then die. God sent Elijah to her, and to be honest with you, at first read my bleeding heart is irritated with him. Because when she tells him her plan and that she doesn't have any bread for him, he said, "Great. Go ahead, bake that last loaf—but first, make a small one for me. Bring it to me, and then make something for yourselves."

Wait, wait, wait. Hold up.

Did this holy man just roll up on a widow, talking all, "I know you're starving and down to your last resources, but make me some bread"? Because I know this tale too well, when a corrupt minister exploits the poor for his special project or building campaign (where like 1 percent of the money actually goes where the video says it will), and this makes Elijah suspect to me. Which is why we have to read the Bible in its context and not only through ours. What Elijah said next is the game changer. "For this is what the LORD, the God of Israel, says: 'The jar of flour will not be used up and the jug of oil will not run dry until the day the LORD sends rain on the land'" (1 Kings 17:14 NIV).

There's a miracle in her midst.

Elijah prophesied a promise, and in order to receive that promise, she had to trust and obey. As difficult as it must have been for her to follow through on his request, she made him a meal, and the promise was fulfilled. Turns out Elijah was not prophe-lying, and God made good on the word he had given to the widow through the prophet. She had to take her last and give it first. Can you imagine how terrifying that must have been? Even if she was at the end of her rope, given over to the fate caused by the socioeconomic factors of her day, she still chose to hope, to trust God for the impossible.

135

Faithful to his word to care for orphans and widows throughout the entire famine, God never let the flour run out. The oil never ran dry. What she thought would be her last meal at the table was the first of many more, as she gained new life and new hope in her choice to trust God. Sometime later (we have no idea how long), her son got sick and died, and she cried out to the prophet in verse 17, "Man of God, what do you have against me? Seriously, what in the Sam Hill is going on around here?" (English Standard Ashley Version).

> Some time later the son of the woman who owned the house became ill. He grew worse and worse, and finally stopped breathing. She said to Elijah, "What do you have against me, man of God? Did you come to remind me of my sin and kill my son?"
>
> "Give me your son," Elijah replied. He took him from her arms, carried him to the upper room where he was staying, and laid him on his bed. Then he cried out to the LORD, "LORD my God, have you brought tragedy even on this widow I am staying with, by causing her son to die?" Then he stretched himself out on the boy three times and cried out to the LORD, "LORD my God, let this boy's life return to him!"
>
> The LORD heard Elijah's cry, and the boy's life returned to him, and he lived. Elijah picked up the child and carried him down from the room into the house. He gave him to his mother and said, "Look, your son is alive!"
>
> Then the woman said to Elijah, "Now I know that you are a man of God and that the word of the LORD from your mouth is the truth." (vv. 17–24 NIV)

In her grief and anger, she cried out to Elijah. Elijah did the same to God, and when he prayed, her son came back to life. The widow's table, where she had chosen to give when it would have been easier to withhold, continued to bring the miracle of life to her household.

The table is not only a place for miracles but also a pathway to purpose, where courage is required.

As a mom of two young boys, I am inspired by the story of Daniel and his best friends Shadrach, Meshach, and Abednego to trust that young men can hold fast to truth, no matter how enticing this world is. I'm encouraged for you and me as well. King Nebuchadnezzar, in Babylon, decided to kidnap the best and brightest youth in Israel and indoctrinate them into the customs of his kingdom with the hopes that he could raise up the next generation to perpetuate Babylonian values and beliefs. When these teenage boys arrived in Babylon with their fierce love and loyalty for the God of Israel and were given the opportunity to eat from the king's table, they said no, asking their caretaker (more like their master) if they could just eat vegetables and drink water.

He liked them, so he said, "Fine, but if you end up weaker than the others, that'll be a problem, so keep that in mind." Daniel's like, "Okay, got it, you'll kill us if it doesn't work out. Cool. We're still gonna do it though," and the boys began to fast and trust God to teach them how to uphold their values while also operating within the culture of Babylon.

The best food on the planet was before them—meats, delicacies, and other rich, delicious foods—and these boys somehow recognized that if they didn't keep control over their appetites, their appetites would take control over them. It took serious gumption to say no, and if teenagers in 500-something BC were the same as the ones I know today, they were likely teased and ridiculed by their peers for skipping the T-bone in aged balsamic, because what slave in their right mind would do that? **I'll tell you who: one who is not a slave in his mind.**

At the end of their training, these boys were bigger, better, and badder than the rest, and the king favored them and promoted them. They continued to serve God and pray to him and him only, even when they were under the penalty of death (all four were thrown into a fire, which they survived, and Daniel was thrown into a lion's den, which he was rescued from). These young men grew up in the Babylonian Empire remaining deeply devoted to God and forsaking anything and everything that would conflict with their love for him. Through every trial, God was faithful, and the men remained courageous and true and continued to earn promotion after promotion, gaining influence in the kingdom. And it all started at the table.

The table is a pathway to purpose, reminding us who we are and what we're living for, especially when we gather around it with friends who spur us on in our bravery.

Finally, the table is a catalyst to peace.

The final table we'll examine is the Last Supper with Jesus and his disciples, in John 13–17, where he washed their feet, they took communion together, and Jesus gave them instruction on what feels like an impossible kind of love, the fruit of that love, and a prayer for unity. The gathering feels like Jesus was carving out a respite from the turmoil of the day, a solution to chaos. He offered them peace in a troubled world where they likely struggled to find it. Jesus said, "I am leaving you with a gift—peace of mind and heart. And the peace I give is a gift the world cannot give. So don't be troubled or afraid" (John 14:27). Racism, sexism, nationalism, political and religious alliances operating to control people, poverty, greed, disease, cultures clashing, slavery, refugee crises. . . . their world had run amok. (Sound familiar?) Plus, on top of that landscape, Jesus's crucifixion was merely days away, and the disciples would be losing the very person they had placed all their hope and future in. Besides his words, what could possibly comfort them through this?

A meal. They broke bread, turning to peace, to love, as a solution to society's atrocities and to their personal pain, fears, and insecurities. Jesus took the time to remind them what's true. Over these five chapters, he spoke to them lovingly, offering direction for the days to come, encouragement for the hardship ahead, and words of wisdom for how to live together in community and how to operate in Jesus's name. "A new command I give you: Love one another. As I have loved you, so you must love one another. By this everyone will know that you are my disciples, if you love one another" (13:34–35 NIV).

When he finished pouring himself out for the ones he loved, and for us today, who are still reading and dedicating ourselves to his words, he was arrested, tried, convicted, and crucified. I can't help but reflect on the meals of Jesus. He has so much to teach us through the table. As we discovered in chapter 5, he was always eating with others, and not just his friends but also people he didn't really like that much—and people some of us wouldn't be caught dead eating with. From the religious leaders who manipulated and oppressed others, to the tax collectors who were hustling all the neighbors, to the women society considered second-rate, to the outsiders nobody wanted to eat with, to the five thousand who needed to be fed from the miracle of multiplication through a tiny basket of leftovers.

Food has the power to heal, nourish, and restore us.

My mama demonstrated this reprieve through food weekly. I remember entering my childhood home after school to the scents of cinnamon sticks simmering on the stove and pot roast cooking in the oven, because even though my mom worked several jobs, she made sure there was dinner on the table. When the fragrance of her love filled my nostrils, something within me settled. The big, bad world out there and my issues, problems, and pain seemed to shrink inside the house that love built. When we sat to eat her life-giving meal, I didn't think about anything except how delicious it was and that we were cared for, and in the moment, that was enough.

I wonder if that was Jesus's point, to gently remind us, *My presence is enough. Sit with me at the table and eat. Recline next to me and listen to truth. Share this space and receive love and grace. Be present and let me wash the worry from your mind. Eat and remember that when it gets overwhelmingly hard, devastatingly difficult, or ruthlessly painful, I am with you. I'll never leave you. I am enough for you. It's going to be okay.*

Sister, it's going to be okay. I don't know what you're facing. I don't know what kind of courage is required in the chaos of your life. I don't know who needs to be invited in or kicked out, but if I could sit with you in the presence of our Father, I would remind you that you are loved, that you have something the world needs, and that we aren't the same without you. And may I also encourage you that your table (even if it holds frozen pizza; no one cares) has the power to heal and restore, to reach and rescue, to bring justice and miracles, to discover purpose and courage, to unify and empower, to settle and still.

> *Love well, like your Savior, and when you don't*
> *know what else to do, share a meal.*

My prayer is not for them alone. I pray also for those who will believe in me through their message, that all of them may be one, Father, just as you are in me and I am in you. May they also be in us so that the world may believe that you have sent me. I have given them the glory that you gave me, that they may be one as we are one—I in them and you in me—so that they may be brought to complete unity. Then the world will know that you sent me and have loved them even as you have loved me. (John 17:20–23 NIV)

RISE, *Truth* TELLER

- What the devil meant to destroy you, God has used, and is using, for your good (Gen. 50).
- Our highest and best connection is not through an email, text message, comment, or direct message. It's face-to-face, together in our need.
- The table is a pathway for justice (Jael and Esther).
- The table brings freedom and the miracle of life.
- The table is a pathway to purpose and a catalyst to peace.

- Love well, like your Savior, and when you don't know what else to do, share a meal.

TELL THE *Truth*

- What's your story with the table? Has it played a key role in your life? Why or why not?
- How often do you get to sit face-to-face with others? Why do we need that connection more than a digital one?
- What do you think of Jael's and Esther's stories? Can you see a way for God to use your ordinary moments of character to offer others justice and freedom?
- The miracle of life at the table is powerfully told through the widow's story. Have you ever been skeptical of any wisdom or direction you received that could lead to life? What did you do? If it was safe to do so, how did you decide to trust?
- Have you ever had an "Aha!" moment at the table with friends, coworkers, or family? Did that point you toward purpose or fill you with courage?
- Jesus used the Last Supper with his disciples to instill peace. Has the dinner table represented peace for you, or chaos? What is your takeaway from Jesus's leadership at that meal?

eight

THE TRUTH ABOUT AGGRESSION

A Little Old-Fashioned Truth Telling

You aren't alive if you aren't in need.

Dr. Henry Cloud, *Safe People*

While we gain incredible strength from the tables where we nourish ourselves, we do have to leave our homes, houses of worship, and favorite places to dine and operate in the real world . . . where it is hard out here for the humans, okay? To cope, our western culture seems to place a significant amount of glory on perfection. Magazine spreads are airbrushed straight into impossible standards. Pinterest is always taking us to the next level of "not good enough." (What has happened to kids' birthday parties is atrocious. Why tho?) Other people make us feel like we'd better come correct or not come at all. We also place an enormous amount of unnecessary pressure on ourselves to get it right and do it right and be right nearly

100 percent of the time. And don't even get me started on body image, where some of us feel like we need a nip and tuck, a waistband thingamajig, maybe some implants, and a ridiculous diet so that the outside can cover up what's happening inside.

I understand why we do this. The fear of not being accepted keeps us from being fully ourselves, from showing up in our glorious mess and being present. It's no wonder that we pretend and perform. It's basic survival in this circus. It's easier to wear a mask than tell it like it is. Reality is sometimes too hard, and honestly, by the time we're ready to share it, life has piled up so high that it would take time we don't have, trust we're not ready to give, and a whole lot of help to unpack it all.

Have you ever really thought about all the things you experience in the span of a day or a week that you don't even think to process with others? Do you ever wonder why you feel fatigued, or anxious, or irritated for (at first glance) no reason at all? Me too—and to stay sane, I have to pause and recount the small interactions and thoughts that add up to my "death by a thousand cuts" emotions.

Have you heard of the term *microaggression*? Webster's defines the word as a comment or action that subtly and often unconsciously or unintentionally expresses a prejudiced attitude toward a member of a marginalized group.* While this word is often appropriately applied in the context of race and ethnicity, I contend that women have to put up with microaggressions on the regular: catcalling, resting B-face jokes, "she must be on her period" vibes, working full-time and also taking care of everything and everyone at home, famous abusers suffering

*Merriam-Webster, s.v. "microaggression," accessed March 20, 2019, https://www.merriam-webster.com/dictionary/microaggression.

no consequences for their actions triggering memories of our own experiences . . . you get the drift.

These repeated daily attacks, no matter how small they seem, add up over time, increasing anxiety, stress, and fear. Our worldview can skew to the negative, and we may struggle to trust or to resist bitterness and a constant sense of irritation with those closest to us as we experience a loss of control and a sense of helplessness about stopping the microaggressions.

These things matter to our emotional wellbeing and our mental health.

Whap! It was the loudest smack I'd ever heard. There was a little boy, no more than four, holding a toy truck and crying in the middle of the sidewalk, next to a very tall teenager who had just been struck and was standing with his jaw clenched. He looked like he was trying to be tough but it was clear he was holding back tears. The boys' mother looked stressed and angry as she yelled at both kids to get into the car waiting to pick them up.

My heart jumped into my throat. It is never okay to abuse a child under any circumstances. At the same time, I thought about how often I'd lost my temper. Was this woman all alone raising her boys? What had happened to lead her to that smack in the street? Was mental illness an issue for her? What had she buried deep inside herself that, if she could release it in a healthy way, would enable her to respond differently to difficulties?

It wasn't even 9:00 a.m., and I'd only made it a block from our house. I'd spent a chunk of time that morning calling 311 to report our negligent landlord; this time, for the electricity that had been flipping off and on for close to thirty days. Weary, discouraged, and a little afraid of getting smacked myself if I interfered, I kept walking toward the train station.

I wondered, as I boarded the subway to work, how often we bear witness to pain, or experience it ourselves, and stuff it all inside, with no real way of getting it back out again. What I witnessed and how I responded that morning are not uncommon for people everywhere. Maybe we don't see violence and aggression up close on a daily basis, but we know what it looks like and feels like, and often, instead of acknowledging the pain, we push right past it. We keep going.

Sitting on the train with my eyes closed, I reflected back only a week, to the shooting of a young man right outside our window. I was in bed and so was my mom, and we both heard the gunshots. We ran into the hallway at the same time, and I texted my neighbor to ask her what she heard. Firecrackers are not unusual for the kids in our community, so I hoped our assumptions were wrong. But when we heard the screaming, we knew the truth.

I was tired that day and had decided to cancel the plans we'd had with our kids that would have put us walking down the street near the time of the shooting. Cody, who had kept these plans on behalf of our family, came up out of the subway just five minutes after the shooting, and walked up on the young man writhing in pain just as the ambulance arrived. When he reached home, Cody looked shell-shocked, and we sat without speaking for a while before we turned on Hulu and tried to settle ourselves.

How do we just go on, like the unimaginable didn't just happen?

Jesus, be near! How can we ever be fully present and vulnerable in a world like this? When it's so hard out there, how can we avoid shifting into perfectionism, pretending and performing, acting like everything is okay?

Later that evening, I spent some time writing and processing how many incidents like this happened in a day, a week. Tears filled my eyes as I realized just how much aggression I have buried alive in order to survive. Memories began to flash through my mind like microfilm, and I landed on another recent painful memory, during my already traumatic labor experience.

―――――――――――

At the birth of our second son, there was a man in the hospital who was responsible for the paperwork. I was in transition (which is the part in the movies where there is cursing, weeping, and gnashing of teeth), so I couldn't really do any paperwork, and the intake staff had forced Cody and me to separate, sending me to wait in triage (Yes, you are reading that right. Triage.), where I had to undress myself, even though my contractions were so close I could barely sit or stand for more than sixty seconds. As I was lying in the hospital gown, with nothing else on, alone, this administrator came walking in, which he was not supposed to do, and asked me for paperwork. He could have asked my husband, but he didn't. He came in and saw me exposed. He did that twice while I was in triage, and again while I was in the delivery room. That time, I shouted, "Can somebody please get him the hell out of here?!" I didn't even get to explain to my husband that this was the third time he had come in, lurking where he shouldn't have been.

Do you know this fool also had the nerve to walk slowly by my patient room on a completely different floor while I was breastfeeding my son, peering in like he had a right to look? There's a period of time, because of room-sharing at the hospital where we delivered our second son, that partners cannot spend the night with the new moms and babies. Cody left for a few hours to sleep on the couch at his office, and guess when that dude decided to come through? You guessed it: while my husband was gone.

Why didn't I report him? you might be asking. Well, if I did report this man, whose name I still don't know, who was going to fire him? No one. Who would do something on my behalf? No one. And the honest-to-God real reason I didn't want to come forward: Who wants to spend the first few hours of their birth experience filing a report, identifying the perp, and having even more people coming in and out, checking and asking for things? No one. Plus, I didn't want to wake my baby boy, so I said nothing.

In some ways, and maybe you'd join me in this feeling, it is what it is. Part of taking up space in this world is knowing that this is what it means to be female. It means a lot worse than this, and I know I don't have to tell you that.

The world is not safe or kind to women.

The levels of anxiety and depression women face are absolutely baffling, and I think underneath it all, we're angry, sisters. Does that resonate with you? I've found it can be hard to even identify with rage, as a woman, because we've been taught that it's normal to live through things like I just shared. That anger isn't appropriate for "nice girls," and that we should stuff everything somewhere nobody can see it. The problem with that logic is our incredible potential to turn all that violence inward, hurting ourselves and in turn, hurting others. Stuff the shame of sexual abuse. Stuff the red cheeks during the meeting with men who laugh at innuendos. Stuff the pain of being the only woman of color present when a racist joke gets made. Stuff the catcalling, lurking, creeping perverts who feel it is their inherent right as a male to invade any and all of our space. Stuff the dreams in our heart that are suffering at the hands of men and women who want to control our personal pursuits and narrative.

No, you can't preach on this platform. No, you can't speak up about that issue. No, you don't have the right to be here. No, you don't get equal pay for equal work. No, you may not say what needs to be said and do what needs to be done. No, you cannot do better than the rest of us.

Sister, yes you can.

Nobody owns your story. You'd better rise up, get up, and speak up. Against unspeakable odds and impossible opposition, we need you to take your place.

How many dreams have we built for others? How many times have we given ourselves away too cheaply? How many salaries do we pay with our hard-earned tax dollars? How many people benefit from our existence without the least amount of resistance? How many times have we been told to wait, to stand down, to accept the lesser vision and dream than the one for which we were created?

Here's what I know: women are resilient. We are tenacious, powerful, and beautiful. Our sisterhood is generous and loving, ferocious and brilliant. We are made in the image of God, one-of-a-kind, wonderful in all of our ways, and we are hilarious and full of sass to boot. We have survived since the beginning, and somehow, we're still here.

You're still here. I'm still here.

There's a story from the Bible in Matthew 15 that aids me in dealing with the societal stress we find ourselves immersed in daily. Jesus spoke truth and challenged the religious leaders who were holding all the power and trying to control the narrative of others for their own advantage. This passage of Scripture is especially meaningful to me because Jesus not only called the actions of individuals into question but also challenged the entire structure of their organization. The individual decisions these men made together impacted the community at large. They were responsible for the lack of equity and love of neighbor in their sphere of influence.

But of course they didn't see it that way.

Then the Pharisees and religious scholars came from Jerusalem and approached Jesus with this question: "Why do your disciples ignore the traditions of our elders? For example, they don't ceremonially wash their hands before they eat bread."

Jesus answered, "And why do you ignore the commandment of God because of your traditions? For didn't God say, 'Honor your father and mother,' and, 'Whoever abuses or insults his father or mother must be put to death'?

"But you teach that it's permissible to say to your parents when they are in financial need, 'Whatever gift you would have received from me I can keep for myself, since I dedicated it as an offering to God.' This doesn't honor your father or mother. And you have elevated your tradition above the words of God. Frauds and hypocrites! Isaiah described you perfectly when he said:

These people honor me only with their words,
for their hearts are so very distant from me.

They pretend to worship me,
  but their worship is nothing more
  than the empty traditions of men."

Then Jesus turned to the crowd and said, "Come, listen and open your heart to understand. What truly contaminates a person is not what he puts into his mouth but what comes out of his mouth. That's what makes people defiled."

Then his disciples approached him and said, "Don't you know that what you just said offended the Pharisees?"

Jesus replied, "Every plant that my heavenly Father didn't plant is destined to be uprooted. Stay away from them, for they're nothing more than blind guides. Do you know what happens when a blind man pretends to guide another blind man? They both stumble into a ditch!"

Peter spoke up and said, "Will you explain to us what you mean by your parable?"

Jesus said, "Even after all that I've taught you, you still remain clueless? Is it hard to understand that whatever you eat enters the stomach only to pass out into the sewer? But what comes out of your mouth reveals the core of your heart. Words can pollute, not food. You will find living within an impure heart evil ideas, murderous thoughts, adultery, sexual immorality, theft, lies, and slander. That's what pollutes a person. Eating with un-washed hands doesn't defile anyone." (Matt. 15:1–20 TPT)

The Pharisees were the religious leaders of the day, and they were about as crooked as a dog's hind leg. They set impossible cultural standards for religion and pretended (key word) they were perfect, as if they were able to uphold those standards personally, which made people feel inferior to them and fostered an elitist culture that fed on vulnerabilities and brokenness.

151

PSA: nobody is character flaw–free, but if the powers that be create an atmosphere where everyone is jockeying for approval, recognition, and perfection, then people will remain trapped in isolation and shame, because nothing we do, or are for that matter, will ever be good enough.

In their culture and our own, true community is hindered by competition and jealousy, because the prize is winning, becoming one of "them," and being right or perfect. Real relationship is stifled, because the controlling leadership does not want people to freely be who they are created to be, perfectly imperfect, esteemed and dignified simply for being created in God's image. The power remains at the top of the pyramid rather than shared in mutual respect among all people, who deserve to have a voice of power, a vote in deciding on the creation of a culture that is fair and just for all. (Honestly, why have we settled for this Ponzi scheme for so long? There are so many more of us on the bottom of this power structure.)

In Matthew 15, Jesus was like, *enough already*. The Pharisees obeyed on paper, but really they bent the Bible to commit injustices, even against their own fathers and mothers. They were frauds pretending and performing but all the time committing crimes against society and God and holding people to a standard they didn't keep.

Then Jesus turned to the crowd, who had been rejected by these religious leaders (remember, Jesus's disciples were the ones no other rabbi picked), and said, "Every plant that my heavenly Father didn't plant is destined to be uprooted. Stay away from them, for they're nothing more than blind guides. Do you know what happens when a blind man pretends to guide another blind man? They both stumble into a ditch!" (vv. 13–14).

Basically, he's saying, "Look, these men aren't from God and they aren't following God, and if you keep following them and trying to be like them, you'll be blind and half dead in the ditch too." (For the record, I added the half dead part, but I think it's true.)

I wonder if there was an audible gasp from the religious leaders and the crowd. And I wonder if there were rebels and outlaws like me who said things like, "Yeah, that's right! I told y'all—better let 'em know, Jesus! Say *that!*" (Probably not, since women back then had no rights and got stoned for just about anything, but I bet the tea-sipping time, after this particular truth-telling Jesus moment, was especially active. I can hear it now. "Girrrrrrrl . . ." Head nods. Mmmm hmmms.)

The point is, bad things have to be uprooted. Lies, injustices, microaggressions, abuse, and pain will kill us if they sit in us too long. If each of these things doesn't pass through a process, like digestion that gets rid of waste, it rots, and when it rots, it corrupts our perspective, our words, and our behavior. That's what Jesus was saying. And he's coming with the facts—not just what needs to be done but what will be done.

"Every plant that my heavenly Father didn't plant is destined to be uprooted."

You'd best believe it was their destiny to be uprooted, these fake spiritual hoodwinkers. These lying men, who gave the people a false and downright mean impression of who God is, of who and how he loves, who also abused people financially and spiritually and did it all in the name of God. Jesus came at them with the thunder, reminding them that God would not stand for it.

To be honest, this chapter of Matthew scares me as a religious leader, and this Scripture is also the exact relief I need. On the one hand, I feel afraid because of my own tendency toward perfection, to do all the right things without the right heart. I can see how the center of my soul has the potential to rot internally as I wade through the waters of pride, control, and anger. It's too easy to see people and situations through the lens of what I really want instead of what is best, and it's tempting to hide it all behind perfectionism, pretending, and performing. Just like the religious leaders. We need grace to know we need forgiveness, that it's okay to not be okay, and to release and expel pain, before pride or rage, control or sorrow can swallow our souls.

On the other hand, I feel relieved because of the confidence God gives me through the words of Jesus, that it is better to be honest than perfect. He always tells it like it is. He didn't try to spare their feelings. The men were hurting people and needed to be publicly called out for the harm they caused. I feel encouraged by Christ's example that the systemic injustices that bind us as women, as people, will not stand eternally. Corruption does not win in the end. It will not always be this way, even if I have to live this way for the rest of my life. We have an advocate in Jesus. He has placed his heart in men and women, and we are better together.

Knowing this truth, I am empowered by Jesus to orient my life around freedom. I can, as an individual, fight for wholeness, and I can, with the help of others, stand against injustice. Both/and. Imagine what could happen if we each decided to turn and peacefully refuse to accept the harmful status quo. I picture the religious leaders lording their power, their rules, and their standards over the heads of vulnerable people, and in the face of that I picture a greater power. People rising from the ashes having made peace with themselves and God, who are determined to walk right through the invisible walls and ceilings constructed to contain and control people. Outside those barriers is space. Room for us all in our brokenness and diversity, in our issues and problems and pain.

We're all down here living this thing out together, and we've got to start working together for the greater good. As we do, we can continue to step out of controlling environments and into equitable spaces where everyone has a voice and a vote. We can rise to take our place and give others permission to do the same. We must build a more just world, unencumbered by the weights of racism, sexism, classism, materialism, militarism, consumerism, or any other *ism*. One relationship at a time, we can and will overcome.

As I close this chapter, it's important for me to say that men are not our enemy.

Based on what I've shared, you might think that's my story, but it is not. Heck yes, I am angry, but I choose to channel that anger into a healthy commitment to helping both genders come together to make a difference. A predator's soul is as torn as the prey's, and for a person to reject their own humanity in order to verbally, emotionally, physically, or sexually abuse a child or adult means they are in the sunken place. For real. And there is hope and transformation for these evils through just accountability and a long recovery process.

I am married to the most freedom-filled, Jesus-loving lover of people I know. I am raising two sons and I pray, by the mercy and lovingkindness of Jesus, that they will understand their place in the world and use their privilege and power to arrest injustice and release every captive. I pray every day that they will walk in humility and grace, that generosity and kindness will lead their lives, and that they will honor people in the way of Christ, regardless of gender, ethnicity, country of origin, or economic status.

The future is female, yes, and we've needed the movement to tip the scales. I pray they keep shifting toward greater diversity and opportunity for those who were formerly excluded—and still I believe we are better together. God created humanity in his image, male and female he created us, and said it was very good. He purposed us for redemption and enabled us by his Spirit to be transformed, and as we challenge ourselves to hold space for what we each add as value, for what we subtract in our brokenness, we recognize that we need each other to carry out the full work of justice that is needed on the earth. We need each other to show up—present, humble, and honest—and we need it now more than ever.

Perfection is a farce. Aggression is undeniable. We need each other to break the power of fear and control. It's time for us to drop the act and get real.

RISE, *Truth* TELLER

- "You aren't alive if you aren't in need." Dr. Henry Cloud

- Microaggressions matter to our emotional well-being and our mental health.
- A complete stranger or anyone who does not have your consent has no right to your time, your body, or your mind.
- The world is not safe or kind to women.
- Nobody owns your story. You'd better rise up, get up, and speak up. Against unspeakable odds and impossible opposition, we need you to take your place.
- Nobody is character flaw–free.
- Jesus empowers us to orient our lives around freedom.
- Perfection is a farce. Aggression is undeniable. It's time for us to drop the act and get real.

TELL THE *Truth*

- How does the ideal of perfection impact you personally as well as women of all ages in your life?
- Describe a time when you didn't feel like you were good enough. What contributed to that feeling?
- What microaggressions did you experience this week? Did you notice them or brush them aside as normal? What did you do with your feelings?
- "The world is not safe or kind to women." Do you agree with this statement? From your personal experience, why or why not?
- When you read Matthew 15, how does Jesus's response to the Pharisees' hypocrisy make you feel? Do you think Jesus tells it like it is?

- How do you feel about "the future is female" movement?
- Do you agree that men are not our enemy? How can we constructively contribute to both genders being "better together"?

Part Three

LIVE WITH
HOLY GUMPTION

nine

THE TRUTH ABOUT POWER

Integrity over Image

Love is or it ain't. Thin love ain't love at all.

Toni Morrison, *Beloved*

As we recognize our role as image bearers of God, in the way of Jesus, it's important to remember that we are still human beings with this flesh on our bones beckoning us to do all kinds of things that do not come recommended by the FDA, FBI, or friends who love us. Perhaps the most dangerous of all is when we give in to our pride so that we value our image over our integrity.

We are a people obsessed with image. Sure, we've been drinking the Kool-Aid and letting magazines, television, family members, and authority figures indoctrinate us for decades about our looks being our primary source of value—but have mercy on our souls; with social media in the mix it sure is hard to stay saved. It's like we just can't stop tooting our own horns and posting pictures that capture the very best of our lives. Cultivating our top nine on Instagram (Yes, you know I do it. Well, I try to do it, but it's not that good, to be honest), hiding behind our image on Facebook (whether it's angry, super sad, happy, happy, happy, or complaint after complaint), accusing everyone on Twitter (like a train wreck I can't stop watching).

I think we do this because there's no way to really photograph the hard stuff. When life falls apart and we're crying in our cornflakes—or are in the middle of being a complete jerk or acting really selfish—we don't exactly stop to take a selfie. "Meltdown due to my own selfishness. #real."

This can feel like a Millennial generation thing, to hear the older folks tell it, but the truth is these older folks are just as serious about keeping the bad stuff hidden as younger folks are. There's no age limit on hiding and pretending. In fact, our obsession with image started back at the fall, when Adam and Eve hid in the garden. God asked, "Where are you?" and they were like, "Oh, we're just over here," hiding and pretending they didn't just get hustled by that wily, rotten serpent. Their instinct was to protect their image, covering themselves in fig leaves and acting like nothing happened in order to keep secrets from God. "We're fine, everything's fine! All good here, sir, thanks for asking!" (Code for: I'M NOT FINE. I'M REALLY NOT FINE. EVERYTHING. IS. NOT. FINE.)

In Genesis 1, God exhaled creation with his breath. He looked around at his work and said it was good. Then "God created human beings in his own image. In the image of God he created them; male and female he created them" (Gen .1:27). He blessed them and said to them, "Be fruitful and multiply. Fill the earth and govern it. Reign over the fish in the sea, the birds

in the sky, and all the animals that scurry along the ground"
(v. 28; take that, serpent).

Then the book of Genesis carries on in such a way that *Jerry
Springer* looks like redemptive television programming. As a
small example, Noah built an ark in chapters 7–9, and the whole
earth was flooded for a (potentially much-needed) do-over, then
chapter 10 lists all the descendants of Noah. Next we move on
to the people of Babylonia, who wanted to make a name for
themselves, in chapter 11.

> Now the whole world had one language and a common speech.
> As people moved eastward, they found a plain in Shinar and
> settled there. They said to each other, "Come, let's make bricks
> and bake them thoroughly." They used brick instead of stone,
> and tar for mortar. Then they said, "Come, let us build ourselves
> a city, with a tower that reaches to the heavens, so that we may
> make a name for ourselves; otherwise we will be scattered over
> the face of the whole earth."
>
> But the LORD came down to see the city and the tower the
> people were building. The LORD said, "If as one people speak-
> ing the same language they have begun to do this, then nothing
> they plan to do will be impossible for them. Come, let us go
> down and confuse their language so they will not understand
> each other."
>
> So the LORD scattered them from there over all the earth,
> and they stopped building the city. That is why it was called
> Babel—because there the LORD confused the language of the
> whole world. From there the LORD scattered them over the face
> of the whole earth." (11:1–9 NIV)

They found a place and settled there. Who is *they*? Nimrod,
son of Cush the grandson of Noah, was a mighty warrior and

hunter. He established his kingdom, a very large civilization that included Babylon and three other cities in Shinar, and then he went to Assyria, where he built Nineveh and three other cities. Pretty impressive, right?

It's my understanding that these folks did not come to play, and in Shinar they settled and considered themselves, their city, and the dreams they planned to build. Instead of looking outward, they turned their energy inward toward self-sufficiency and self-preservation. Instead of having a unified goal to spread what God had given them throughout the earth, they decided to make a name for themselves. Listen, I am not an Old Testament scholar like Walter Brueggemann (though I recommend his commentary on Genesis to you). However, I don't think it takes much heavy Bible-lifting to know that by settling in Shinar, which was rich with resources, and then constructing a giant tower so people would know how rich and famous they were, these Babylonians had lost the plot. They'd made the will of God secondary to their own. Settling down replaced sending out. The people of Babylonia were actively resisting God's commandment in Genesis 1:28 to fill the earth.

As a little rabbit trail, I wonder if this is how it starts for people like Adolf Hitler and David Duke—an ancient stronghold of pride that upholds things like white supremacy and lies to people, saying, *We're better than the rest of them. We should not be separated from our kind or speak any other languages. It is only people like us that God really loves and blesses. Let's make a name for ourselves and show the rest of the world how good we are! Conquer and eliminate.*

I also think about how so many churches are stagnant, declining, or dying because of an "us four and no more" mentality or a territorial approach to building ministries that keeps all the efforts of its people contained within the community rather than equipping them to effect positive change in the world. How many leaders and organizations are set on building an invisible tower of power in order to look good (not just do good) to those outside who are watching?

> *Goodness gracious, it's scary who we can become*
> *when we make God in our own distorted image.*

What I find interesting about the story in Genesis 11 is that God did not seem upset over their unity. He came down (which I love, because they thought they were really doing something, building a tower to the heavens, and God's like, *Umm, that's real small, but good effort, children*) and said, "Look at them go. With their one language, nothing they plan to do will be impossible for them, so let's confuse their language so they will not understand each other." And he scattered them throughout the earth.

Their unity was a good thing. Their motivation, on the other hand, not so much.

Since God created all humankind in his image, he loves every person. *Spoiler alert: even the ones we might not like!* Or the *ones we're prejudiced against.* In case you've been poorly taught, this story is not about the awesomeness of some kind of Aryan pureblood race (also, they're all kind of inbred, soooo . . .) but about God's will, which he declared in Genesis 1:28 and would declare again over Abraham in Genesis 12:

> Go from your country, your people and your father's household to the land I will show you. I will make you into a great nation, and I will bless you; I will make your name great, and you will

be a blessing. I will bless those who bless you, and whoever curses you I will curse; and all peoples on earth will be blessed through you. (vv. 1–3 NIV)

Their blatant disobedience was the thing that God had to hinder. Their decision to be internally motivated by their own will and not his, their need to make a name for themselves rather than honor God's name, and their laser-like focus on image over integrity were a problem for our Creator. And because he's good, he refused to let them destroy themselves by operating in unity about the wrong things. He needed them unified about his command, which was and is to fill the earth.

Unity isn't good when you're united about the wrong things.

On that note, doesn't Jesus's promise to destroy the temple in Luke 21:5–6 make so much more sense now? As we've already learned, the Pharisees and religious leaders of his day were unified in their efforts—but they were oppressing and crushing the very image of God in the people they tried to manipulate and control. They pretended to be perfect and valued their image over their integrity. The religious leaders thought they were serving God, but they were really serving themselves and their own agenda to take and keep power.

It almost feels like God, from the very beginning, is telling us repeatedly that we are not here to build elaborate buildings or to make a name for ourselves. We're not here to hoard our personal and communal resources. We are here to bless, to go, and to send. It's not about us. *Fill the earth with the image and the presence of God, who is good.* We are not created to fill the earth with our image, because it won't hold up, but we are here to bear the image of God so that people will understand that the Creator of the universe is an untamable, mysterious, ferociously good God simply by looking at our life. Also, we're all still working on how to be the same person we are when no one's looking as we are in every other environment, so we've got to be honest enough to say that we don't have what it takes to be in total control of everything and everyone.

God's integrity, on the other hand, does hold up. He is the same no matter who is watching, and he doesn't need to toot his own horn or build a tower for everyone to see, because he is God . . . who made the whole universe. He paints the sky at dusk and dawn. He created human life with his words. He redeemed our life from the pit by sending his own son to sacrifice himself so we could be included. He, not we, deserves all honor, praise, and glory.

The primary issue with the Babylonian mentality is that it encourages us to make ourselves bigger than God.

The Babylonian people may have been scattered that day but their rally cry lives on, ancient, subtle, and evil. The devil has no new tricks, but pride is his best one and we fall for it all the time. We see him in our greed and conquering, our self-pity and pretending, our smoke and mirrors, our self-absorption and obsession, and we must fight against it relentlessly. It is in the air we breathe, and without actively confessing and living in the truth and light of God's love and holiness, we are simply becoming like the world around us: hungry for fame, desperate to be known and remembered. If we're not careful, whatever we are building—even in Jesus's name—can be more about us and our platform than about him and his glory.

Let's just be real about it: even with Jesus, pride is a central issue in our lives. Personally, pride has kept me bound up in unforgiveness. Pride has hindered relationships in my life. Pride has given birth to control, anger, fear, insecurity, and jealousy in my heart. Pride has kept me at odds with the will of God. At different times in my life, pride has made my image, my desire, my insecurity, and my intellect my god. I can think of nothing more destructive to the purpose of God in our lives and in the lives of others than pride.

I believe we build an image because we are searching for significance. To help our search, Ephesians 1:11–12 in *The Message* version says, "It's in Christ that we find out who we are and what we are living for. Long before we first heard of Christ and got our hopes up, he had his eye on us, had designs on us for glorious living, part of the overall purpose he is working out in everything and everyone." When we haven't yet learned how to be found in Christ, we look to find ourselves in our relationship with another person, our career, the clothes we wear, the car we drive, our waist size, our Instagram likes, being better than other people, or proving ourselves to someone in our past because that makes us feel significant, like we matter. I'm not against any of those things, but if our motivation is to exalt our image above our integrity, then we've rooted our pursuits in pride.

This spirit that desires fame, attention, and power thrives in our misunderstanding of our value and identity, and we hurt ourselves and others when we seek to craft an image that impresses people. In this spirit, people become a commodity, a means to an end, rather than a community, the means through which the will of God is possible.

There's an old saying that you've likely heard or read somewhere: "Humility is not thinking less of yourself; it's thinking of yourself less." When we think of prideful people, we tend to demonize them a bit, as if pride belongs to a certain personality type. But whether we think we are the best of the best or the worst of the worst, we're still hoping to win first place at something—self-importance or self-pity both find their roots in pride.

I get it. I like to be in control, and I am tempted to make a name for myself at the expense of the will of God and the lives of others. I easily construct idols to distract me from the rest and peace I find in God's grace. I'm at my worst when I am building and controlling my life without the help of God and without listening to healthy people who care more about the truth than how good I think I look to others. I don't know if I know a more terrible god than me. Do you feel that way? It's only when I humble myself to ask God for help with the mess I've made that he helps me destroy the idols, accept his way, and choose integrity over image.

What are some of your idols that need to be consistently torn down?

I'll go first. My iPhone is at the top of the list. I wake up with that thing, go to bed with that thing, and my increasingly bad posture shows you how much I depend on that thing all day, every day. With that phone, I am busy and important! I am getting things done. I am responding and reacting, problem-solving and connecting. But I am also missing the moment far too often and disconnecting from my family regularly, and I am ruled by the needs of others who expect me to respond in a ridiculously short amount of time. My brain pushes past sheer exhaustion because of the stimulation of the screen. I need an intervention. Or a flip phone. Maybe both.

Pride is another idol of mine. If I'm not careful, it's my way or the highway, and my perspective is obviously the right one—and hello, look at this good thing we've started! It's amazing! Let's just build it higher and higher and admire what we've done instead of spreading it like a dandelion you blow on to make a wish, leaving the outcomes of the seed for God alone to see. Or I can get so stuck in my head about how bad things are, or how bad I am, and either way, if I'm wallowing in self-absorption or self-pity, again, the root of it is pride. Look at me, I'm the best! Look at me, I'm the worst! Either is still making me bigger than God and his grace. And that is the root of a lot of sin, and I (we) have need for repentance.

How do we tear down our idols? Well, it's not that easy, but in an effort to keep it simple, we can follow this three-step process: Recognize. Repent. Reflect.

One, recognize. Recognize the sin in order to grieve the sin. We cannot heal from anything we refuse to acknowledge. It's like an alcoholic who has two drinks per night saying there is no problem. Living in denial will not allow us to walk in freedom. Our statements of "It's not that bad," "I'm not as bad as that guy," and "That's not who I really am," turn into "Wow, it is that bad," "It doesn't matter what they are doing; it matters what I am doing," and "Yep, that's exactly who I am."

We're often terrified to see ourselves as we are, and we avoid it like the plague, but we are liberated when we look—really look—at ourselves. There's freedom when we take all the masks off, when we put down the armor of our image and bare our souls before our Creator, sorrowful and sorry for what we have done and who we have become. A simple, "I'm sorry, God. Will you forgive me?" can change everything. In that humble place, we are greeted with grace by the Lord who heals and helps us. We are also introduced to who we really are in his eyes. We learn who he says we are. Yes, we are sinners, *and* we are more than conquerors in Christ Jesus. The riches of his kindness leads us to repentance. And in Christ we find out who we are and what we're living for. Life in the Spirit with God relieves pressure; it does not add it. Freedom comes when we recognize our sin and our need for a Savior.

> For I know my transgressions,
> And my sin is ever before me.
> Against You, You only, I have sinned
> And done what is evil in Your sight,
> So that You are justified when You speak
> And blameless when You judge. (Ps. 51:3–4 NASB)

Two, repent. I say this often, especially concerning reconciliation, but "Sorry" doesn't mean jack unless it comes with changed behavior. Repentance means to change, to turn from our way and walk in the way of Jesus. My ways can be destructive, even when I seem okay, just like the people of Babylonia. They were building in unity but they were off, and what they were building would have destroyed them without God's intervention. When we repent, we commit to change, to surrender our way and accept a better way.

For example, do you know how many hours I gave Instagram last week? Twelve, according to an app I have that tracks my screen time. What am I supposed to do with that, beside hide my head in shame and misery? Instead, I'll confess to you, which is step one of repentance. I'm concerned, frankly, and I should be. But that's not enough to stop me on its own, no more than a porn addict is going to stop watching because they see how many hours they are wasting on selfish pleasure and the objectification of men and women made in God's image.

What can stop me is realizing how little time I gave this week to reading my Bible, worshiping God, and connecting with people on my commute. And under stress I mindlessly have a scroll to quiet my anxieties or check out a bit, even at home with my family. Not to mention the things I hoped to do but didn't, yet somehow I managed to find twelve hours for Instagram. Living in an echo chamber is also a concern, and although I am deeply committed to diversity of thought, and my feeds for the most part reflect this, groupthink is still a danger to me on the internet. All of this is destructive and has effects as well on my brain, my psyche (FOMO, comparison, what's cool), and my eyesight from looking at this tiny phone so much.

What is the better way? What can I replace this behavior with? It is second-rate connection, and yes, while I love the opportunity to influence and encourage people with these incredible social media tools, I don't need twelve hours on Insta to do that. Connection, in real time, is the better way. So I need a plan to change, to act out my repentance. As I've heard it said many times, "If you fail to plan, you are planning to fail."

My plan is to move my phone from my bedside so that when I wake up in the middle of the night I have no easy access to

Instagram and will read my Kindle instead. On my commute home, because I have already stared at a laptop all day, I plan to keep my phone in my purse or backpack and practice sitting still, doing nothing, and if there's a chance to converse with a neighbor on the subway, I'll be available. If not, I will rest my eyes, sit up straight, and give my brain a break from technology. At home, I need to leave my phone in my purse or backpack and unburden myself with my husband, as is appropriate to do so, and spend time talking, listening, and playing with our kids as we go through the dinner, bath, and bedtime routine.

Next, I will tell my plan to a few people who will ask me how it's going and be there when I mess up. When we have only practiced one way, that way is cemented in our mind as *the* way, and as much as we think willpower will sustain us as we try to change, it does not have staying power. We all need a little help from our friends.

I am also happy to report that this week I decreased to four hours per week on Instagram and social media just from doing what I planned!

Three, reflect. Once we have recognized our sin and repented, creating a plan to help us walk out a better way and sharing that plan with a few trusted people for regular check-ins and help, we then carve out time for reflection. A daily or at least weekly time for inventory. How are we really doing? Did we fall back into any of our old habits or ways of doing things? If so, why? Were we unusually stressed? Did someone from our past contact us? Is there a bill we can't pay? Did we hurt someone with our words or actions? What caused it?

Reflection helps us understand why we do what we do, but even better, it also gives us space for an exchange. *God, in this place I acknowledge the struggle, and I exhale my anger/ grief/anxiety/hurt/pride and inhale your love/joy/peace/healing/ humility. Lord, I acknowledge that I don't have what I need or what it takes to walk in the better way, but with your help, and the help of those who love me, nothing is impossible for me. I exchange my way for your way. I trust you, Lord, and I surrender.* Through reflection, we meditate on and receive God's truth.

> May these words of my mouth and this meditation of
> my heart
> be pleasing in your sight,
> LORD, my Rock and my Redeemer. (Ps. 19:14 NIV)

And look, I used my iPhone as an example because it's really what I'm dealing with right now, and on the surface it doesn't look too bad, but any addiction is one too many. Maybe the issue is deeper for you. Maybe you hate someone because of the color of their skin and you struggle to admit that you're a racist, or you're having an affair, or you lack integrity in your finances or you're doing shady stuff at work.

Friend, there's a better way.

I don't know what your sin is, but no sin is special so you're not alone—we are all sinners saved by grace. Repentance is not a one-time thing; it's a regular, habitual rhythm in the life of a believer. If you struggle with sin, you're normal. Salvation is not a magic pill; it's an invitation to follow in the way of Jesus, something we cannot perfect on this side of heaven. The practice of repentance works for us all, especially in our temptation to hold all power and control through valuing our image over integrity. Through this practice of asking for and receiving forgiveness from God, we are transformed daily and renewed in his image, walking in a better way as we journey with Jesus.

We don't have to live as the culture tells us, in or out of the church. You can tear down every idol in your life, again and again. Jesus is the way, and he will lead you, step-by-step, as you humble yourself and trust in him.

RISE, *Truth* TELLER

- Unity isn't good when you're united about the wrong things.
- The issue with the Babylonian mentality is that it encourages us to make ourselves bigger than God.
- If we're not careful, whatever we are building—even in Jesus's name—can be more about us and our platform than about him and his glory.
- Let's just be real about it: even if we're following Jesus, pride is a central issue in our lives.
- We build an image because we are searching for significance.
- When we think of prideful people we tend to demonize them a bit, as if pride belongs to a certain personality type. Self-importance or self-pity both find their roots in pride.
- A simple plan for change: Recognize. Repent. Reflect. There is a better way.

TELL THE *Truth*

- Have you witnessed a group in society that was unified about the wrong things? What do you think about that?
- Have you ever been part of a group that was unified about the wrong things? If you did, how did you leave that situation?
- What does it mean to make ourselves bigger than God? Have you ever done that?
- Do you resonate with pride being a central issue in the life of every person? Why or why not?
- What's your experience with repentance? Do you find the three-step plan for change helpful?
- Is there an area of your life that you know needs to change? When you search the Scriptures, do you see a better way for that area?

ten

THE TRUTH ABOUT RECONCILIATION

When You Don't Like the Skin You're In

I can't stand life because I was born a suspect.

Chris Rock

We've had nine chapters together, so I think it's time for me to tell you about the seven warrants I've had out for my arrest. You're reading that right. Seven. It all started when I was driving down Washington Street on my way to school in Eden, North Carolina, as a sixteen-year-old who refused to get up on time and still had hot rollers in her hair. I was shifting gears, eating breakfast, and applying red Estée Lauder lipstick—when out of nowhere, sirens!

What! Why, though?

I froze, terrified, and in fact had only applied red lipstick to my top lip when the Eden police officer tapped on my window and asked if I knew why he'd stopped me. I was not lying when I said, "No, sir."

"You were doing 50 in a 35."

"Oh. I didn't realize I was speeding!" (That was true, for the record. I did know that the rollers in my hair were not quite ready to come out yet, though.)

"License and registration, please."

I handed over the goods, and he went back to his car. I sat there, scared out of my mind. Boy, was I ever relieved when he came back, handed me a warning ticket, and said that he knew my dad. I thanked him, plus the host of heaven, and went on my way.

I don't know exactly how many times this happened in my hometown, but close to a dozen, if I'm estimating, without anyone actually writing me a ticket.

When I went off to college, I started driving on something called a freeway beltline, and apparently those state troopers were not there to play games, because almost immediately I got my first speeding ticket! And not two weeks later I was returning my car to the parking lot on campus, most definitely driving 35 in a 15, and the campus police stopped me.

Okay, here's what you need to know: in my defense, I thought campus police were a step above mall cops. Like, I had no idea they could actually write tickets, so when he pulled me over and let me know he was writing me a ticket, I laughed hysterically, like I was high, and said, "You can't write me a ticket! You're the campus police!"

Well, he did not appreciate that, and he wrote my behind a serious ticket.

A week later, I was on my way home to visit my family and got another ticket in a neighboring town where they had nothing better to do than catch young people speeding. In under a month I had three tickets, and as sure as the sun will shine, I was about as dumb as a brick concerning these matters. I didn't know you could go to court for tickets! Appear before a judge for speeding? What kind of sense did that make? For some reason, the third ticket had the earliest court date, and since I was at school I didn't show up.

Y'all, why did my mother call me, talking about how "The sheriff came to get you today." Say what! Can you repeat what you said, because I died and was resurrected. Did you say the sheriff came to get me?

Yes, yes he did. That same neighboring town also liked putting young people in jail for speeding, I guess.

I was lucky enough to have a few friends at the courthouse, through family connections, and the judge dismissed my case. Shew, one down! I realized this was serious business, paid the mall cop, errr, campus police ticket, and then made a plan to show up in court for the state trooper situation.

I dressed myself in a three-piece suit (from 5-7-9, I'm sure) and put a fake diamond ring on my finger so it looked like I belonged to someone (which tells you so much about my psyche and way of being in the world at that time). When they called my name to come before the beautiful, pregnant judge, I walked right up to her bench—and was shocked when the bailiff came and snatched me up. Did you know that you cannot walk up to the judge who has just called your name? You did? Well, I didn't. You may not walk up to a judge—ever. You may not breathe, or speak, or do anything at all. I was clueless!

I backed up, because the bailiff backed me up, and then the judge asked me about the ticket and I told her honestly what happened, though I also embellished a few life details that made me look in crisis (I was, though, just not for the reasons I gave her) and unable to afford the cost of the ticket and the court fees. The court had mercy on me and dropped the most expensive ones, then sent me upstairs to pay the processing fee.

And so we don't die together in these details, I had four more warrants in Los Angeles County, for driving with a suspended license, for missing court dates, and for parking tickets, plus one warrant in another state for speeding.

Why would anyone miss a court date, after they know better? I'm glad you asked. Because it costs money to sit in court all day, not only because when I didn't work, I didn't get paid, but also because I had to drive an hour to downtown LA (once I went to the wrong courthouse, also; that was fun) and pay to park. And when you can't miss a day of work, or your hourly employer won't let you, what do you do?

Risk your job, or not go to court?

I chose to not go to court. I would often play it off with people in my life like it didn't bother me, but the truth is, I was bothered, yet I knew I couldn't miss work. Depending on your economic bracket, you might've been around this mountain as many times as I have and already know that the expensive ticket, if left unpaid, only grows exorbitantly with time. Usually, when I finally did get to court and started dealing with the tickets or license, I owed the city between $1,500 and $2,000 every time.

Some people really don't understand why poor people don't "just get it together," do what they are supposed to do, follow the law, and so forth. Have you ever tried to navigate the court system without money? (Jesus, be a fence!) Until you pay the court, you can't go to the DMV, which means you can't drive, and in Los Angeles, without proper public transportation, this is a problem because that means you can't get to work. Parking tickets basically double if you miss their due date, and by then they are an unaffordable bill for many people, so ignoring them is necessary—not because poor people like debt but because if paycheck-to-paycheck is your way of life, an extra $200 might as well be a million, and if you were forced to choose between keeping the lights on and paying a parking ticket, well, what would you pick?

Not to shirk my responsibilities as a law-abiding citizen, because that matters, but as I grew older and more removed from my teenage experience in my hometown, living on my own in an urban city, below the poverty line and eating peanut butter for every meal, I felt like every parking ticket, every DMV complication, and every little extra thing would sink me.

What if the law isn't fair? How are the rules just if they only work for certain economic brackets? Why is it okay for two people with the same issue to be penalized differently based on whether or not they can afford to pay the court fees?

The last time I was pulled over, I was singing at the top of my lungs to Fred Hammond, minding my own business at a traffic light. When I tell you I was supremely obedient to all traffic laws by this point, I mean it. No more than seven miles over the speed limit, no rolling stops, no U-turns if prohibited. I didn't want to ever go to court again. Ever. The officers stopped me because I had a taillight out. I handed them my license, not thinking a thing about it, and when they came back they asked me to step out of the car. Apparently, the courthouse and the DMV don't always communicate (no one is shocked, I am sure), and didn't realize an old court matter had already been resolved.

The officer had a trainee with him, and he impounded my car and left me on the side of the street with my laundry, waiting for Cody to pick me up. We had just started officially dating, so here was his big chance to decide he could do better. But Cody laughed instead and took me home. He was unbothered, and this made me want to marry him and have his babies (and drive an SUV, of course). The next day, my mom drove me to the courthouse, the DMV, and the tow lot because she is the MVP of my life. I got the matter sorted and the taillight fixed. I was making more money and had savings, and for the first time didn't feel paralyzed by sheer terror of the court system. I could handle it all the first time, mail in the fix-it tickets, and be done with the whole thing.

Money changed everything.

Bryan Stevenson, founder and director of the Equal Justice Initiative and author of an absolute must-read book, *Just Mercy*, has often said, "We have a system of justice that treats you better if you're rich and guilty than if you're poor and innocent. Wealth—not culpability—shapes outcomes."[*]

Has anything more true ever been said? The first time I heard Bryan speak, I was helping to host the Justice Conference in LA, and every hair on my neck stood at attention and I felt like my skin was on fire. God had already been stirring my heart about the issue of mass incarceration in America, and after

---

[*]See, for example, "Bryan Stevenson Talks to Oprah about Why We Need to Abolish the Death Penalty," *EJI*, November 28, 2015, https://eji.org/news/bryan-stevenson-tells-oprah-winfrey-why-we-should-abolish-death-penalty.

that, I knew there was no way I could not do something. I had no idea what, but I knew it was time.

────────

After I had reached out to several city leaders expressing my desire to serve, an LAPD chaplain followed up with me, talking about God's perfect timing because he had just started a program in the detention centers at two local precincts called the Nehemiah Project. He invited me to become a chaplain. I was pregnant and a female and they still let me serve.

Through this ministry, we prayed with people who had just been arrested and brought to holding and were waiting for release or arraignment—and this is when I realized just how lucky I was. Almost everyone I prayed for had been arrested for one of these things: gangbanging, prostituting, being a John who had purchased sex, being homeless, or having a warrant out for their arrest. There's a lot to say about the deeper individual and communal injustices around all of those things, but the warrants began to open my eyes in a way that kept me up at night.

I prayed with a beautiful mother who had absolutely no reason for being in jail. She literally looked like she had been on her lunch break from the office when she was pulled over. She had a two-year-old at home with her mother, and her eyes filled with tears as she told me about her tickets and her missed court date due to work, and that when they pulled her over the police arrested her. She was worried about her job and her son. I saw myself in her, but out of all seven of my warrants (save the sheriff determined to jail me), I never once was arrested, and in fact several times I had been let completely off the hook and simply told to take care of the outstanding court stuff.

The only difference between us was our skin color.

And this happened again, and again, and again, and again. Immigrants and people of color with warrants just like mine, in jail—now with the burden of both their tickets and bail. Serving my brothers and sisters who were arrested and detained changed my life and gave me insight and understanding that I will never stop thanking God for. For instance, our cash money bail system perpetuates poverty.

In addition to the 1.6 million people incarcerated in federal and state prisons, there are 646,000 people locked up in more than 3,000 local jails throughout the United States, 70 percent of whom are being held pretrial—meaning they have not yet been convicted of a crime and are legally presumed innocent. One reason that this unconvicted population is so large is because our country largely has a system of money bail, in which the constitutional principle of "innocent until proven guilty" only really applies to the well-off. With money bail, defendants are required to pay a certain amount of money as a pledged guarantee they will attend future court hearings. If they are unable to come up with the money either personally or through a commercial bail bondsman, they can be incarcerated from their arrest until their case is resolved or dismissed in court.*

I have no idea what happened to any of the folks we prayed with; all we had was that moment to invite the presence of God to minister to them and give them courage and grace. However, I can still see some of their faces, and I will tell you where they don't belong—jail.

*Bernadette Rabuy and Daniel Kopf, "Detaining the Poor: How Money Bail Perpetuates an Endless Cycle of Poverty and Jail Time," *Prison Policy Initiative*, May 10, 2016, https://www.prisonpolicy.org/reports/incomejails.html.

Before *privilege* was a curse word, God graciously tended to mine. All that time, I would hit my knees and thank God for his grace every time I didn't get a ticket or suffer any real consequences besides debt and time spent. Then I realized grace didn't have much to do with it, but *white* sure did. And not just any white but six-feet-tall, skinny, blonde, green-eyed white.

Some of you know exactly what I am talking about because you live this, every moment of every single day. You know what it means to live conscious of your skin color, or the country you came from, or the religion you choose to practice. You don't have the luxury to not think about your place in the world.

And some of you want to close this book.

Before you stop reading because you don't want to talk about race and criminal justice and politics, please consider journeying with me here. I know it's not easy for us to listen to each other. I know we live in a nation of red and blue, left and right, alternative facts and fake news, but we are created to build bridges with our truth telling, not burn them down, and this is what I intend to do here, with you.

If you believe you are created in the image of God, and you also believe that he has created every person in his image, then you must contend with any resistance you feel toward anyone who is not like you, as must I; otherwise, how will we ever be transformed? My dear sister, Dr. Mary Glenn, often says, "Remember that this person is beloved of Christ, and that is your starting point."

Beloved of Christ, stay with me here, I beg you, not just for my friends who so desperately need your advocacy and care but for your own soul, which is fractured without the entire body present and participating.

> Now if the foot should say, "Because I am not a hand, I do not belong to the body," it would not for that reason stop being part of the body. And if the ear should say, "Because I am not an eye, I do not belong to the body," it would not for that reason stop being part of the body. If the whole body were an eye, where would the sense of hearing be? If the whole body were an ear, where would the sense of smell be? But in fact God has placed the parts in the body, every one of them, just as he wanted them to be. If they were all one part, where would the body be? As it is, there are many parts, but one body.
>
> The eye cannot say to the hand, "I don't need you!" And the head cannot say to the feet, "I don't need you!" *On the contrary, those parts of the body that seem to be weaker are indispensable, and the parts that we think are less honorable we treat with special honor. And the parts that are unpresentable are treated with special modesty, while our presentable parts need no special treatment. But God has put the body together, giving greater honor to the parts that lacked it, so that there should be no division in the body, but that its parts should have equal concern for each other. If one part suffers, every part suffers with it; if one part is honored, every part rejoices with it.* (1 Cor. 12:15–26 NIV, emphasis added)

My friend, can you take a moment to read the verses in italics again? Go ahead, I'll wait. What do you think about them? How do they speak to you?

For me, this passage is a reminder that we each consider parts of humanity to be weaker or less honorable. Maybe we more easily discard or dismiss immigrants who are at our borders, or blondes who we assume are dumb anyway, or overweight people, or men who make us clutch our purse when they pass, or children and teenagers, or people with disabilities, or the elderly in our midst. It is in our human nature to rise to some sense of superiority over someone, to avoid and ignore certain people. But this passage of Scripture is saying to us that *these are the indispensable people.* Our presentable parts need no special treatment, but God has put the body together (all of us), giving greater honor to the parts that lacked it so that there would be no division in the body but rather its parts should have equal concern for each other. Just because it's not happening to you doesn't mean that it's not happening.

The apostle Paul is communicating that we should give greater honor to the parts that lack it, especially those likely to be overlooked, forgotten, despised, misunderstood, or seen with the utmost disdain, *so that* there would be no division.

And so that we would have equal concern for each other. Why? Because of this bold truth: we are all made in God's image, and at the foot of the cross the ground is level. No one is inferior or superior to anyone else—we all stand side by side before Jesus. We're just walking each other home.

Friends, what do we have to be so haughty about? Let's take just one of these things: race. It is a social construct, created at the beginning of the transatlantic slave trade to enslave and oppress people of color and to keep all the money and the power at the top with a select few folks. Before that time, people were part of tribes and communities, cities and nations.* You've been reduced to the color of your skin, and

*For more reading on this, a great place to start is Ta-Nehisi Coates, "What We Mean When We Say 'Race Is a Social Construct," *Atlantic*, May 15, 2013,

I to mine. What is our heritage? Before I was white, I was the descendant of immigrants from Europe, mostly British, Irish, and Swiss, with a little Scandinavian. Making my ethnicity a color is entirely reductive, although I understand to migrate into the United States it was necessary for European Americans to be white or white passing. That was the only way in, outside the horrific brutality of forced migration through slavery or through indentured servitude. Our skin color doesn't make us better, or less, than anybody else. God made us with the beautiful skin we have. Each of us is precious and unique in his sight.

Power and greed around the issue of race especially (but gender as well) has been hustling us far too long, making us mad at each other instead of mad at corruption, redlining, voter suppression, poverty, poor education, and unequal healthcare access. Those with power and resources make the rules of society, and sometimes it can feel like we're down here dying on the field while they are living large in the box seats, watching us kill ourselves while they get rich at our expense.

Please, I am too tired to fool with these lies.

You know what I wrote when I filled out my son's NY Department of Education forms? They asked me his ethnicity, followed by these choices: White, Black, Asian American, Native American, Hispanic, Other. I crossed out white and black, and

https://www.theatlantic.com/national/archive/2013/05/what-we-mean-when-we -say-race-is-a-social-construct/275872/; J. Kameron Carter, _Race: A Theological Account_ (Oxford: Oxford University Press, 2008); Lisa Sharon Harper, _The Very Good Gospel: How Everything Wrong Can Be Made Right_ (Colorado Springs: Waterbrook Press, 2016).

wrote, "These are colors, not ethnicities!" And I decided not to answer the question, because we are Caucasian mutts anyway, and it would take forever to list out all of that.

I grew up in an all-black daycare with my little brother and loved it. We lived at the YMCA and the library after school, and the Y was full of kids who didn't look like us, and for the longest time I didn't even notice we were different. We had the same economic bracket, the same teachers and coaches, and very similar experiences, and in many ways we were the same.

I used to say something I really regret, now that I better understand systems, which is "I don't see color."

First of all, yes, I do. I don't look at someone's outfit and think, *Nah, I can't see it. No color there!* There is nothing wrong with acknowledging differences, and it has become essential for us to realize that our skin color, based on the history of our country and the way we move in the world, has a profound effect on our life experience.

There are names I will never be called. No one worries I will steal when I come into their store. People give me the benefit of the doubt. I have very little trouble getting a job. Of course, there is an intersection of race and gender, so experiencing sexism and getting shut down in meetings and being asked if I am somebody's secretary are just part of being female, but I am not marginalized or tokenized to the degree of my friends who are people of color.

After working in community development and serving in jails and churches, I can assure you that skin color is seen, and it matters.

189

It matters to nonwhite immigrants living in our communities. It matters to children at the border, traumatized in detention centers. It matters to mothers raising black sons, who fear for their lives as they watch children such as Tamir Rice and Jordan Edwards being killed senselessly. It matters to men of color and the women who love them, who fear that a routine traffic stop will end their life or that one petty crime could result in their incarceration for years and a permanent stain on their record that could revoke their right to vote, to receive help, and to find work. It matters to the families of African Americans and Latin Americans, who make up about 32 percent of the entire United States population but represent 56 percent of the prison population. It matters because white people use drugs at the same rate as people of color, but people of color are six times more likely to be charged for drug use than white people. It matters because in 2012 alone, our nation spent $81 billion (yes, billion) on corrections. It matters because 1 in every 37 adults in the United States is under some form of correctional supervision.[*]

It matters to women at the hospital whose symptoms are ignored and overlooked, to black women in the labor ward who are three to four times more likely to die during childbirth. In fact, the United States ranks 32nd out of 35 of the wealthiest countries on Earth for infant death rates, down from 12th in 1960. The *New York Times* published a thoroughly accurate article concerning this issue, and I want to share a direct quote with you.

> Black infants in America are now more than twice as likely to die as white infants—11.3 per 1,000 black babies, compared with 4.9 per 1,000 white babies . . . —a racial disparity that is

[*]NAACP, "Criminal Justice Fact Sheet," accessed March 7, 2019, https://www.naacp.org/criminal-justice-fact-sheet/.

actually wider than in 1850, 15 years before the end of slavery, when most black women were considered chattel. . . .

This tragedy of black infant mortality is intimately intertwined with another tragedy: a crisis of death and near death in black mothers themselves. The United States is one of only 13 countries in the world where the rate of maternal mortality—the death of a woman related to pregnancy or childbirth up to a year after the end of pregnancy—is now worse than it was 25 years ago. . . . Black women are three to four times as likely to die from pregnancy-related causes as their white counterparts . . . a disproportionate rate that is higher than that of Mexico, where nearly half the population lives in poverty—and as with infants, the high numbers for black women drive the national numbers.*

I'm not even cracking the tip of the iceberg with these issues. Maybe you're like me and you have family members who grew up in the Rust Belt or in the South and suffered from extreme poverty even as white people. If so you might know what it's like to be called a redneck, or trailer trash, just because of the part of town you grew up in or the trailer park you called home. You know exactly what it's like to have a person with more means, power, and authority assume what your life is all about, decide what your capacity and intellect might be, and determine to keep you hidden and silent. Maybe you know the sting of food stamps and free lunches. It's highly likely, because Caucasian people receive more government benefits than any other race in America. But no one really talks about that in the media or anywhere else.

*Linda Villarosa, "Why America's Black Mothers and Babies Are in a Life-or-Death Crisis," *New York Times*, April 11, 2018, https://www.nytimes.com/2018/04/11/magazine/black-mothers-babies-death-maternal-mortality.html.

Perhaps you know the struggle that it is to share the pain of poverty, or you're still suffering from the effects of trauma and abuse, and that has turned you into an "All lives matter," "Build a wall," "If the children didn't want to get separated from their parents, then they shouldn't have come," or "I'm not privileged, never have been," kind of person. *What about us? Why isn't anyone fighting for us?*

Can I share something with you? Your pain matters too. Your heart is precious to God, and he loves you. He dwells in the trailer parks the same way he dwells in the jails. He has been with you every time another child made fun of you in the lunch line. He was there when a family member used pure meanness to knock you down for no reason. He was present in the grocery line as your family tried to figure out how to pay for things that are not included in that government money, like toilet paper and tampons. He has seen it all. He fights for you too.

We don't fade away into the background when we acknowledge the severe disparity and inequity between races. We don't invalidate our own experience by validating someone else's. But we do grow in empathy and understanding, and we do have the opportunity to share our own story as well, because we all need to hear the truth about these experiences. *Why* we think what we think and do what we do matters. We need to hear each other outside of the polarization of cable news and social media.

So share your story. Go first or go second, but just don't go in the comments section.

We have so much more in common than we have realized. It is time to allow the Lord to knit us together, to cross our great divides, so that we will have equal concern for each other. If one part suffers, every part suffers with it; if one part is honored, every part rejoices with it.

This is not going away. Justice is not a trend. It is the heart of the Father. Without equal concern for each other (all of the others), we will not be reconciled. I also think the bridge we need to build is shorter than we imagine. We are picturing an ocean between us but there's nothing but a little creek. Step in and step over. We need to rise to this moment in history and determine that we will love each other in the way of Jesus, who sees our gender, race, culture, economic situation, and social status and withholds nothing from us. We are all seated together with Christ, in equity and equality, and it's time we get on with the business of heaven and decide to not only get along but work together for a more just society.

We can do better, and we must.

RISE, *Truth* TELLER

- Memorize 1 Corinthians 12:22–26.
- "We have a system of justice that treats you better if you're rich and guilty than if you're poor and innocent. Wealth—not culpability—shapes outcomes." Bryan Stevenson
- "I don't see color" is not a helpful or true statement. Skin color is seen, and it matters.

- Making our ethnicity a color is entirely reductive.
- Validating someone else's experience does not invalidate our own.
- The bridge we need to build is shorter than we imagine. We are picturing an ocean between us and there's nothing but a little creek. Step in and step over.
- We can do better, and we must.

TELL THE *Truth*

- What has been your experience with police interactions? How about the court system? How has that impacted you or people you care about?
- Do you think money changes things for people's lived experience in society? If so, how does it change the way they live in the world? If not, why not?
- What do you know about incarceration in America? Were you surprised by some of the statistics? What is your reaction to those facts?
- Have you ever said, "I don't see color," or been the recipient of that statement? Looking back, how does that make you feel?
- Do you agree that power and greed shape race as a social construct? Why or why not?
- "Black Lives Matter" or "All Lives Matter"? Gently explore what you think of these two statements, and why.
- Are there any parts of humanity you view as easy to dismiss or discard? What are you going to do about your capacity to do so?

eleven

THE TRUTH ABOUT PROPHETS

Christians Who Shout on Social Media

> Our culture is competent to implement almost any-
> thing and to imagine almost nothing. It is the vocation
> of the prophet to keep alive the ministry of imagi-
> nation, to keep on conjuring and proposing futures
> alternative to the single one the king wants to urge as
> the only thinkable one.
>
> Walter Brueggemann, *The Prophetic Imagination*

You know why it's hard to get along? Because people are selfish. For real. Okay, I told you I would tell you about the one
time I regret telling my story, and it was on Christian television.
Other than the Bishop T. D. Jakes and Joyce Meyer programs,
I've never really fooled with it, mostly because cherubs and gold
and royal purple everything are not in my version of heaven;
it's always creeped me out a little.

So this show calls me up, having seen my story on a website, and they ask me if they can send a film crew to share my story on their channel. It felt like a no-brainer for me, because I love to see women set free from their past by sharing God's grace and redemption in my life.

The first clue that I had made a serious mistake was when the producer arrived and asked me to have one dark and sad-looking outfit and one colorful bright outfit ready for the shoot, then kept asking me to go deeper with details and feelings that were inappropriate to share with the public.

I also should have sniffed out the Christian-cheese that came with them wanting to film me walking in a woodsy park, but I had no idea that they would really take this thing to the next level.

They hired an actress to play me, like this was *America's Most Wanted*, and her dance moves in the flashback scene were almost more embarrassing to me than the full segment. Also, I don't drink beer. Truth is in the details, people! The network chose to cut all of the present-day material, which meant they focused solely on the trauma of my story and completely exploited the drama of what I had gone through, using me as filler for another show where they interview guests.

It was both humiliating and hilarious. I learned a valuable lesson that day, which is to watch the show before you say yes to being on it, because this was another day, another dollar for that crew, but for me, millions of people tuned in and fed off my past with no idea of how beautifully God was shaping my future. The gift of my embarrassment was a personal understanding of how it feels to have my story exploited for someone else's message, program, or sermon series, and my slow realization that I just don't like American Christian culture.

Yeah, I said it.

Some of y'all have also been thinking that for the longest time, and when you saw Gandhi's quote on Pinterest, "I like your Christ. I do not like your Christians. Your Christians are so unlike your Christ," you pinned it and thought about adding it to your #sundayselfie.

I remember when I was in college, and people would invite me to the FCA meetings to come and get "saved," I would roll my eyes like a NeNe Leakes gif because I got saved in 1988, which these Christians would've known if they'd bothered to ask me any questions at all about my life. I was born again and baptized and acting like a wild hyena, and they were born again and baptized and acting like Pharisees, so **you know who really needs Jesus? The Christians.**

Girl, you know it's true. Ooh, ooh, ooh.

I was able to have that story segment removed from the network channel and YouTube, and the sweet woman who took my phone call apologized and told me that the producer was no longer at the network. Maybe that's good, but I don't know if it helped stop the big machine that eats people up and spits them out (for free, by the way, no one is paid to do these stories, at least not regular people; we're just supposed to be honored and thankful to exploit ourselves for the greater good).

———————

My wrestle with the church, with other Christians, has been difficult. At one point, my husband and I weren't sure we'd ever attend church again. We thought to ourselves, *We already have an amazing community. We're serving in our city in meaningful ways. We'll open our home, give our money away, love the (literal) hell out of people and let them love us the same, and this will be our church*. No drama, no hierarchy, no dealing with emotional vampires, no failing under anyone's expectations, no worrying about where our money is going or who is steering the big ship (and if we're about to hit a glacier or not).

So, we didn't go for almost a year. We had one faith community where we could attend anonymously from time to time, and we'd go for the corporate worship experience. To be honest, that's all I really missed.

It was so freeing to just *be*, to enjoy each other on the weekends, to sleep late on Sundays and go to brunch, after years and years of spending our Sundays serving others. I was finding a footing and unlearning the unsustainable pace, replacing it with the unforced rhythms of grace.

Also, I was avoiding church folks like it was my full-time job.

Some people were concerned I was backsliding (although leaving the church does not automatically mean leaving Jesus). Some friends wanted answers I didn't have or time I didn't have the mental energy to give, so we just hunkered down and did our best to journey quietly, with our closest friends and family.

I just needed to breathe, without the machine. To determine if I still loved the church, if I still wanted to be part of the corporate gathering, if it was still worthwhile to build, but perhaps in a different way. We were exploring contemplative forms of worship, and I was devouring books on justice, hungry to see how my faith expression could intersect with my love for just systems. I craved deeper, more meaningful experiences, and began to set the table at home for more conversations and less lectures.

Faith became simple again in that space of sharing life with others, of enjoying my husband and baby, of laughing and crying, processing and transforming. I felt connected to Christ again, more sure of myself, and eventually was able to realize that I still loved the church and wanted to try again.

I looked again to the words of Jesus at Passover in John 13, 15, and 17, when he washed his disciples' feet and shared a last meal. I started to consider how I might more thoughtfully live out his commands. What would bring evidence of his goodness and grace to this world? Jesus said three things.

Love

A new command I give you: Love one another. As I have loved you, so you must love one another. By this everyone will know that you are my disciples, if you love one another. (John 13:34–35 NIV)

Fruit

Remain in me, as I also remain in you. No branch can bear fruit by itself; it must remain in the vine. Neither can you bear fruit unless you remain in me. I am the vine; you are the branches. If you remain in me and I in you, you will bear much fruit; apart from me you can do nothing. If you do not remain in me, you are like a branch that is thrown away and withers; such branches are picked up, thrown into the fire and burned. If you remain in me and my words remain in you, ask whatever you wish, and it will be done for you. This is to my Father's glory, that you bear much fruit, showing yourselves to be my disciples. (15:4–8 NIV)

Unity

I am coming to you now, but I say these things while I am still in the world, so that they may have the full measure of my joy within them. I have given them your word and the world has hated them, for they are not of the world any more than I am of the world. My prayer is not that you take them out of the world but that you protect them from the evil one. They are not of the world, even as I am not of it. Sanctify them by the truth; your word is truth. As you sent me into the world, I have sent them into the world. For them I sanctify myself, that they too may be truly sanctified.

My prayer is not for them alone. I pray also for those who will believe in me through their message, that all of them may be one, Father, just as you are in me and I am in you. May they also be in us so that the world may believe that you have sent me. I have given them the glory that you gave me, that they may be one as we are one—I in them and you in me—so that they may be brought to complete unity. Then the world will know that you sent me and have loved them even as you have loved me. (17:13–23 NIV)

Maybe this is why Gandhi didn't like the Christians! Love, fruit, and unity are not exactly what we're known for. (I can hear the responses now. #notallchristians)

A year into our break from the church, Jesus pulled what I like to call the holy hustle, and somehow we became pastors again, in Manhattan, and God put all that rest to the test. We started serving our new church in the middle of the 2016 presidential election, and it was like entering the Twilight Zone. Christians were going AWOL, shouting on social media, pridefully telling everyone what to do, posting the weirdest prophets from YouTube (which, come on, doesn't that tell us everything we need to know?), and utterly forsaking the gospel of love.

Every week, I was like, *Wait, what in the world did you just say?* I was unfollowing and unfriending because I don't do racists, and I felt more anger than ever at both the silence and the stupidity of the church. I felt disgusted with the spiritual civil war happening in our nation, but I felt pressed to choose a side as well, with my refusal to align myself with nationalists and Alt Right folks (hello, let's not rename the KKK, friends) rallying in Charlottesville, carrying tiki torches and shouting, "You will not replace us!" and "White lives matter!" and "Hail Trump."

In the name of Jesus, no.

As a white pastor who had just made her peace with the church, I couldn't even tell anyone I was a pastor until they knew which side I was on, because the media on all sides were having a field day, and people of color were distraught, heartbroken, and leaving the church left and right—and I just wanted to leave again with them.

What is wrong with us, Jesus? How have we strayed so far from your Word? How can pastors stand in pulpits and say nothing, or tell people how to vote, or declare some random prophecy from YouTube as "Thus saith the Lord"? I mean, what are we really out here doing?

Are we a place for the marginalized? Are we a place for the weary, the broken down, the hurting? Are we a place for the prideful, the greedy, the poor, and the sick? Or are we here to tell people how to think and what to do so that we feel comfortable? Are we here to partner with political leaders to push policies that benefit our agenda? Or are we here to create a more just society for all, regardless of their religious beliefs (as per the actual Constitution)? Do we really have no answers for the raging world around us? Will we work toward solutions? Or will we keep running with our tone deaf teaching series, our little weekly service meetings, and our thoughts and prayers? Do you know how many problems the evangelical church could have solved already if we'd spent even half the amount of time that has gone into planning services on solving an actual problem in the community?

It is time to return to the truth of Jesus and let our life and our faith communities bear witness to that truth.

How do we bear witness? With our love, fruit, and unity. The first way people will know that we are disciples of Jesus is if we love each other. And while the Bible offers constant encouragement to love our neighbor and humanity altogether, Jesus's words in John 13 are specifically to the disciples. "You guys love each other. Even though some of you would argue over the blue in the sky. Even though the temptation to compete and compare overtakes you. Even though you don't come from the same social and economic status. Even though you'd probably never hang out, outside of your relationship with me. Love each other."

I think part of the reason God brought me to New York is because I was always preaching a good word about loving the other—until I actually had to love mine. Oh, Mylanta, was that a tough pill to swallow. It felt like I had to face down all the types of people I had spent a lifetime avoiding, and while NYC seems like a progressive place, let's not forget, the Constitution was drafted here, the Revolutionary War plans were crafted here, and the founding of America as we know it started here, so there are some old demons where we pastor, to say the very least. As I was triggered I resisted, shouting in my soul some psalms about "smiting thee thou mine own enemies, Lord." I was also encouraged by the generous love, understanding, and compassion in our faith community.

And when I felt like throat punching my other, to get those Christian propaganda pushers to hush up in Jesus's name, I felt the Lord whisper, *They are made in my image. Practice what you preach. How will any of you experience transformation without connection?* And this has kept me in relationship with people I would have gladly cut out of my life. His truth has kept me sitting on my fists and kept me from many Facebook arguments, and he has helped me to communicate in such a way that someone who does not agree with me might be interested in hearing what I have to say. (Except sometimes, when I am like, *Nope, not you; I am not fooling with you. Because mental health.*)

God is love, and it will minister to the world if Christians live out his love. If you are patient and kind, not jealous, boastful, proud, or rude; if you are not self-seeking and not easily angered; if you keep no record of wrongs; if you don't delight in evil but rejoice with the truth; if you always protect, always trust, always hope, always persevere (see 1 Cor. 13:4–7). They'll see God in you. They will look with wonder and want to know who he is, because the characteristics the Bible uses to define love are so not normal. Biblical love defies what we see daily, and prophetically points to the perfect way of Christ, who has something more to offer us than what is common.

The second way people will know we are disciples of Jesus is by our bearing fruit. "Remain in me," Jesus urges us in John 15, "because apart from me you can do nothing." Inside each of us is a seed of potential, and that seed will break open into our calling, which is what we were created to do. Calling encapsulates many gifts and talents and abilities, and over our lifetime we'll likely do many things as our vocation and hobbies, with many people in our family, friendships, and networks. The point through it all is to bear fruit. What does that mean? In Christ, we are given the fruit of the Holy Spirit, which is love, joy, peace, patience, kindness, gentleness, goodness, faithfulness, and self-control.

Whatever we do, we are to bear fruit.

If we are dealing with a roommate who won't do the dishes or a colleague who's just not that into us, parenting our children, loving our spouse, tending to a sick family member, serving at church, working as a barista or a CEO, whatever it is, whether we like it or not, we are to bear the fruit of the Holy Spirit. Can you imagine if the two billion people who call themselves Christians on Planet Earth just brought these characteristics to every place we inhabited? Do we even know how radical a witness that would be? How different our workplaces? How wonderful our homes? How beautiful the private and public witness of Christianity if these things were our goal? Bearing fruit shows people that we belong to Jesus.

And the third way people will know we are disciples of Jesus is our unity. Now look, I have nothing in common with some folks and I will testify to that publicly for the sake of the witness of Jesus. Yes and amen. However, we have so much more in common with one another than we might think. In 2002, Stanford published a DNA study; their team analyzed DNA from 1,056 people from fifty-two populations in five major geographic regions of the world—Africa, Eurasia (Europe, the Middle East, Central and South Asia), East Asia, Oceania, and the Americas—and discovered that in our DNA makeup we are 6 percent or less different from one another.* How is it

*Lisa Gannett, "The Human Genome Project," *Stanford Encyclopedia of Philosophy* (Summer 2016), edited by Edward N. Zalta, https://plato.stanford.edu/archives/sum2016/entries/human-genome/.

possible that the tiny sliver of difference we have can separate us so terribly?

I think Jesus knew that when he prayed to the Father not to take us out of the world but to protect us in it, to sanctify us with the truth of God's Word, he knew that we could be unified, because in him we are all one. We can keep the main thing the main thing, with our differences as a key part of the story, and if we say we love him, we will listen to one another, love each other, operate in the fruit of the Spirit toward each other, and maintain mutual respect. Submission to God and to each other will trump our pride and divisiveness.

> *Being love is better than being right,*
> *and it leads us to unity.*

It's worth noting that unity is not assimilation. We see the disciples arguing often in Scripture because they were different from each other, so run for the hills if you enter a space and are ostracized or told to get in line for asking questions, for respectfully disagreeing, or for pointing out the obvious. God is not into groupthink. He makes space for us all, and we also have our Rabbi Jesus, who asked questions and allowed questions and responded to questions with more questions. He is a thinker, and he doesn't mind your mind.

Becoming a Christian doesn't remove our God-given flavor and funk. Jesus sets us free to completely be ourselves. By his grace we are empowered to love as he loves, to bear the fruit of the Holy Spirit in every place, with every person. Through the presence and power of God, we can pursue unity. By this, all of humanity will know we belong to Christ.

RISE, *Truth* TELLER

- It's hard to get along because people, including us, are selfish.
- Sometimes Christians need Jesus the most.
- Our love, our capacity to bear fruit, and our unity are a witness to the truth and life of Jesus.
- Love will minister to the world as people look at our lives in wonder and want to know who God is.
- Whatever we do, we are to bear fruit.
- Being love is better than being right, and it leads us to unity.
- Unity is not assimilation. Becoming a Christian doesn't remove our God-given flavor and funk. Jesus sets us free to be completely ourselves.
- By his grace, we are empowered to love as he loves, to bear the fruit of the Holy Spirit in every place, with every person. Through the presence and power of God, we can pursue unity.

TELL THE *Truth*

- Do you think people are selfish? Do you think you are selfish?
- What is your experience with Christians who need Jesus, who don't practice what they preach?
- Have you ever avoided church folks like it was your full-time job?

- If you are or were a pastor or ministry leader, have you ever taken a break or left your longtime faith community? What was that like for you? Are you still recovering from that time in your life?
- Why is love a stronger minister to the world than hate?
- How do you bear fruit in the ordinary places you go on a daily basis?
- What's the difference between assimilation and unity? Have you ever been ostracized for your curiosity or for speaking the truth?

twelve

THE TRUTH ABOUT JUSTICE

Justice Is Not a Trend

God doesn't have enemies; God has children.

Father Greg Boyle

I can't believe we're here at the end together. We made it, and I'm so thankful for you. I hope that you have been served, challenged, and that you have laughed and released something you were holding on to. You're brilliant, and the hand of God is on your life. He loves you. There are no words that can do justice to that kind of love. It just is, and I pray it rolls down like a river in your wild and beautiful life.

For our last moments together, I want to circle back to something I've already said about justice not being a trend. It's as old as Moses.

When God gave Moses the Ten Commandments for covenant community in Deuteronomy 5–7, the instruction was given to encourage wholeness in the neighborhood. God starts with the command to have no other gods before him. Second, we are not to make an idol in our own image or to worship any other image in the heavens or the earth besides him, and third, we are not to misuse the name of the Lord. These first three commandments inform the remaining seven.

If we can manage to leave God on the throne of our hearts and not build a name for ourselves or worship any images, and if we can avoid misusing his name through letting what we say we believe about Jesus be different from what we do in action, we can probably avoid hurting, abusing, and using people, which is what God commands us to do with commandments four through ten.

Take a Sabbath so you don't use people, because if you don't stop working to rest, you start to feel and act like a machine. Over time, you'll start to see people as commodities rather than those created in the image of God. Honor your parents, so you can have a long, full life, instead of allowing unforgiveness, resentment, or conformity to their ideals instead of God's decide your future.

Don't kill people or have an affair with someone else's spouse. Don't steal or lie about your neighbor. Don't be jealous of what other people have, so you don't end up letting bitterness and envy guide your choices.

This is why Jesus sums up the law in two commands: love God with all your heart, soul, mind, and strength, and love your neighbor as you love yourself (Matt. 22:36–38). At its core, this is justice. When God remains our only obsession, in him we find our identity as sons and daughters in the kingdom of heaven. We carry his presence, and we can live into it and release it here, in our homes, neighborhoods, schools, workplaces—wherever we find ourselves. And shalom, the peace of God, his wholeness—with nothing missing and nothing broken—reigns.

Love hinders our capacity to hurt. When we cherish our neighbor, acknowledging and respecting the image of God in their face, we will be less likely to abuse, neglect, ignore, or destroy their place in the world.

Remember the two billion Christians we mentioned in the last chapter? That's about 30 percent of all the earth's inhabitants. Friends, if we all just lived out Jesus's two simple commands, don't you think we could abolish human trafficking and reduce inequities in education, race, gender, and economics, as well as develop strategies to end global poverty, terrorism, and more? If every Christian alive today focused on worshiping God alone and loving their neighbor, we would light up every corner of the earth!

Christ's love through us could win over gangbangers and pimps and prostitutes and hardheaded, prideful people and abused, discarded children and folks who are apathetic to love because they have never experienced it, and people would begin to get whole and families would be restored, and neighborhoods, cities, and nations could feel the impact. But it sounds too simple, right?

Jesus said that the kingdom of heaven is like a little yeast that a woman worked through sixty pounds of flour until it permeated all the dough (Matt. 13:33). It might feel like we have just a little, but the kingdom of heaven in the person of Christ, living inside of us, is potent and powerful. He modeled this for us. He didn't build a nonprofit or an empire for Christian ministry, but he did go about doing good, and he healed, cared for, and lifted up those whom society devalued or discarded.

Together, with God and with each other, we can permeate this culture with kindness and love and grace, so that people come to know our Father in heaven and begin to follow the way of Jesus. Justice is not a trend; it is the heart of our Father.

Catholic author, poet, and social activist Thomas Merton said, "Our job is to love others without stopping to inquire whether or not they are worthy. That is not our business and, in fact, it is nobody's business. What we are asked to do is to love, and this love itself will render both ourselves and our neighbors worthy."*

In other words, do no harm but take no mess.

As you probably already realized I needed to do, I removed Facebook from my phone this year, because I started hating people I actually like in real life. Suddenly, people started to feel like my enemies. And I'd never had enemies before. Or, at least, they hadn't been popping up in my eyeline on a regular basis. They were easy to deny or avoid. I also didn't have a cell phone at all until 1999, or the internet on my phone until 2009, and I really just used MySpace as my first blog, so there were no digital adversaries in my midst.

I never really cared who hated me until social media created a swirling world of visceral anger, unsolicited advice, and hysterical accusations. I wrote a blog post that went viral once, and the comments section would have made you clutch your pearls and call your priest. When it comes to loving our neighbor, it sort of feels to me that Christians are straying from the basics, especially digitally. The truth is, whatever we feel confident

*Thomas Merton, "Letter to Dorothy Day," as quoted in Stephen Hand, *Catholic Voices in a World on Fire* (Raleigh, NC: Lulu, 2005), 180.

enough to sit behind a screen and post reveals who we really are and what we really think. That's been a little scary to witness over the last several years, as people have gained confidence through saying all kinds of horse poo at home alone and are now starting to publicly act like they were raised in a barn.

Through my blog, I have received many accusations from voices without any tangible connection or relationship to me. One woman, whom I will call Sally, counseled me that "If you truly want to have a Christian voice . . . I entreat you to spend some time at Calvary with Jesus; who you claim to represent." The way she so easily spoke to me as if she were the Author and Finisher of my faith completely disregarded my humanity, my walk with God, and my perspective. Her comments went on at some length and, four or five paragraphs deep, included this gem: "Reading your present work, I can tell you have yet to experience Him, and like many, have a Disneyland version of the real thing!" At that I almost snatched off my earrings and put on my Reeboks to let Sally know what's up. *Listen to me, lady; I have experienced the Lord for myself and seen him work with my impossible circumstances, and I know his healing and deliverance firsthand.* There is not a single plastic thing about my faith; it is raw and real, vulnerable and painful, full of life and joy and hope. Hello, my life message is about taking off the mask and telling the truth!

Throughout her diatribe there was no warmth, no love, and no understanding. I didn't want to get to know Sally; I sure didn't want to visit her church. (Yes, you already know she sent her church's livestream for me to watch, where she has "had the privilege to feast"—whatever that means—why are Christians so weird? No one is walking around talking about feasting on TED Talks, for the love of God.) I didn't invite a dialogue with her, like I have done with many other commenters who completely disagreed with me, because it was clear those were not her intentions. Although I've since made my peace with her naivety, at the time I just wanted her to go away.

I am sure Sally really believed she was acting "In The Service Of The Lord and King," but if her desire was to draw me closer into her truth and her community, it did exactly the opposite. In fact, it felt like she had set herself against me, like an enemy. So if, like Father Greg Boyle says, God only has children, not enemies—then Houston, we have a problem. I wonder if Sally might attend a church that prides itself on being a gatekeeper of truth, where anything else is wrong and must be eliminated or eradicated immediately. I wonder if she has also picked up that mantle.

I don't think commenters like these are seeking to build a relationship, or earn some trust, or help us see another angle; I think they comment to correct, to say that we're wrong and they are right. And since they've got the corner market on truth, what would even be the point in engaging with them?

Has this become the witness of the church? Will we continue to remain this tone deaf with our voice and irresponsible with our place in the world?

I felt embarrassed for every non-Christian, every Christian who is really walking in the love of Jesus, and every Christian who is unsure about belonging to the church who might be visiting my blog, because we are so obvious with our hatred. You're either in or you're out. You're for us or you're against us. You're right or you're wrong. Can we agree in the final moments we have together that we don't have to live this way? Because there's room to live and move in the grey. Faith is nothing without nuance, mystery, and uncertainty.

*We don't all have to agree in order to
live together in community.*

I think reality TV has primed this pump, along with an obsolete, failing education system, churches centered on consumerism, and the organizational structures within our economic system that insist on moving at a glacial speed compared to the rapid pace of technology and evolution of humanity. The power of propaganda and indoctrination is at an all-time high. In many cases, we comment more than we converse. We are more susceptible to allowing people we have no personal relationship with to shape our hearts and minds. Whether they are journalists, hosts on *InfoWars*, scholars, entertainers, preachers, presidents, or political or Instagram stars, we are not privy to their real life, struggle, or hustle, yet we allow them to tell us what to think. (They could be crazy, you know.) On top of that, we're forming our opinions of others and of ourselves based on snapshots of other people's lives. We're missing the whole truth about one another, and it can be so hard to love our neighbor when we don't take the time to get to know them.

*The digital age is changing us, and we
can do nothing to stop it.*

We can only wade in these waters with tenderness and humility, with a willingness to be wrong and a backbone to stand up for what's right. Be encouraged: we are here now, and God is not surprised by the digital age. He's not up in heaven freaking out. He's cheering us on, surrounding us with help, bringing peace in the chaos, restoring hope through the blessed and sacred ordinary.

> Therefore, since we are surrounded by such a great cloud of witnesses, let us throw off everything that hinders and the sin that so easily entangles. And let us run with perseverance the race marked out for us, fixing our eyes on Jesus, the pioneer and perfecter of faith. For the joy set before him he endured the cross, scorning its shame, and sat down at the right hand of the throne of God. Consider him who endured such opposition from sinners, so that you will not grow weary and lose heart. (Heb. 12:1–3 NIV)

How do we rise as truth tellers in a world like this one? One day at a time, seizing the moment, living awake and alive to the people and places right in front of our faces. And we must maintain the audacity, the sheer guts of grace, to own our story, tell it like it is, and live with holy gumption. It has been my greatest honor to journey with you, to serve you as you live your big, beautiful life. You're one of a kind. Never forget that. God took special care when he created you.

Rise, truth teller, rise. The world is waiting, and who knows but that you have come to your position for such a time as this.

RISE, *Truth* TELLER

- "God doesn't have enemies; God has children." Father Greg Boyle

- Love hinders our capacity to hurt.
- Justice is not a trend; it is the heart of our Father.
- Do no harm but take no mess.
- We don't all have to agree to live together in community.
- The digital age is changing us, and we can do nothing to stop it.
- We must maintain the audacity, the sheer guts of grace, to own our story, tell it like it is, and live with holy gumption.
- Rise, truth teller, rise. The world is waiting, and who knows but that you have come to your position for such a time as this.

TELL THE *Truth*

- Do you agree that God doesn't have enemies?
- What does the word *justice* mean to you? Had you ever considered that the Ten Commandments, and Jesus's summation of those commandments, are at the heart of justice?
- How can you do no harm but take no mess?
- What kind of agreement is necessary in community? Can we disagree and still be close to each other?
- How is the digital age changing you? Your thoughts and habits, your perspective and worldview? How will you remain grounded to the truth of God in the digital age?
- How will you rise as a truth teller? What will you do with what you have read?

ACKNOWLEDGMENTS

This book has been in motion since I was little. The pen has been my help and the paper my friend, and the wonderful community who raised me and loved me, alongside those who keep allowing me to participate, to contribute, to show up, are indeed the reason I am who I am.

To the Burleson family, Claudine "Dini," Mike, Braden, and especially my oldest friend, Katie "Burl" Womble; your home gave me hope, bagel pizzas, and a basement full of stories. Your candor has guided me back toward the light, again and again. We are laughing lake rats who expect each other to be honest or else. Grateful doesn't come close to what I feel for you all.

Mrs. Simmons, my first creative writing teacher, who saw through my façade and demanded my best work; you set my feet on this path. Dr. Duane Best, who taught me story through song, and that "discipline is the training that makes punishment unnecessary." I found a place to process my pain in those green walls at JM Morehead High School. Thank you both. Special shout out to Eden, NC, and all my friends from that beautiful town.

To my brother, Jacob Dodson; how did you tolerate your older sister for so many years? Thanks for letting me sneak onto a bunk bed during scary storms. You weren't afraid to tell me the truth when someone or something was controlling or using me. Even though you love country music, thank you for who you are in the world. I love you and the life you're building.

My first pastor, Reverend Freeman, who stood in the back of Grace Baptist Church every Sunday to greet his congregants, held my little hand, received me when I said yes to Jesus for the first time, and baptized me as well. You've been gone a long time, but your love lives on in me.

My beloved great-great-aunt Fairy, I owe you my love of neighbor. Arranging flowers for the altar, opening the church every Sunday, baking cookies, slathering pimento cheese on sandwiches, helping with spelling bees and Scripture memorization, and visiting the sick and the shut-ins nearly every week; you taught me that faith was more than an hour on Sunday, and you prayed me back to Christ when I left him. I can't wait to thank you in heaven.

To my dad, Danny Dodson; thank you for your zest for life and for your wonderful laugh and love for people. I appreciate your cards and kind words of encouragement over the years, and I honor you for who you are.

LaTrayl Adams—sister, where would I even begin? We're still standing! Probably because of all those gospel worship CDs you burned me. You climb over mountains and break through walls, and you inspire me. I am cheering you on, and I love you, always.

To Saleena Lockett, my sister since the first coffee in Silverlake. We've seen so much hell and so much glory, and we're still trusting God. Thank you for the thousand texts we share weekly, and for making me laugh with the memes. You always call a spade a spade, and you see gold no matter what it's buried in. Thank you for being a friend.

Tiffany Bluhm, my partner in crime and fellow Why Tho queen, you have lifted my eyes from the ceilings and walls, to the expansive world of faith that exists outside of every barrier. In motherhood, friendship, purpose, and passion, you inspire me forward. Thank you, dear sister.

My dear Kat Daddy Talley, why did we read the Bible while driving? We have always sought the truth and passionately worshiped Jesus. You're my favorite roommate and my forever friend who watched *Matlock* as a labor of love. Tenderly you asked me, "Why do you give yourself away so cheaply?" and in a moment I saw the truth, and the trajectory of my life changed. Our friendship is a trusted treasure. I love you for life.

Brooke and Brad Wright, oh how your fireplace, songs of worship, and family have sustained us when we thought all was lost. I think of Psalm 27, because I would have lost heart had I not believed that I would see the goodness of the Lord in the land of the living. I have seen God's goodness in you. Thank you for spurring us on.

Dennis and Mia Lamar, we love laughing with you, shouting you down, cheering you on, and praying you through. Your love and passion for Jesus inspire us, and our friendship gives us hope as we persevere each season. Thank you for your love and support.

To the Lake Balboa Ladies, Harmony Grillo, Michelle Lutz, and Lynette Weaver; what a continual safe harbor of vulnerability, honesty, and hilarity we've created. We've suffered together, praised God together, endured the unimaginable together, trusted on nothing but a word, and we always found

God faithful. Thank you for seeing and knowing the worst, for seeing and believing the best. Your love has changed me for the better, for good.

Andi Andrew, you are fire and pure joy, and you have opened the path wide for me to run in what God has for me. Thank you for seeing me, loving me, and being a force for good on the earth. You and Paul have made room for us, and we love you and thank you both, always.

Jana Burson, my brilliant agent, you are excellent at your job, well respected across the industry, and an incredible truth teller. Your guidance and wisdom, your faith and confidence, your passion and worship—my goodness, thank you. I'm holding a book I wrote because of you. May the Lord richly bless your generosity and kindness.

To my acquisitions editor, Rebekah Guzman, who fought for me, believed in me, and never once tried to change me—thank you. Your gentleness, joy, and humility are restoring something in me. To Lindsey Spoolstra, to whom I owe a significant amount of gratitude and grammar; thank you for your attention to detail and for helping me be my best self (#byefelicia). To the rest of the Baker Books team, especially Wendy Wetzel; thank you for being massive but not a machine. Your personal touch and collaborative nature bring peace and joy. I just love you all. Thank you.

To Papa Da, Mamo, Narnie, and Uncle Todd; from the first trip to Texas, you took my breath away with your rich connection and radical generosity. Thank you for your passion for God and your love for our family. God's great grace placed me among you, and I am grateful.

To my mama, Anne Ayers; there are no words to express my gratitude for who you are and all you have done. You are the most influential person in my life, since the womb, and you have cared for me all the way through. Thank you for your great love and sacrifice. It is not lost on me, and I intend to keep doing good with all you have given me. I love you, always.

To my beloved children, Levi and Lucas; you did not sleep nor cooperate often while I wrote this book, and that is why I love you. May you always disrupt the status quo, run headlong into truth, and bring along as many people as you can. You are light and joy in this world; Dad and I treasure you and will remain present to you, no matter what you do or choose.

Finally, to the one my soul loves, Mr. Cody Brooks Abercrombie. You won me with your body rolls and kept me with your ferocious tenderness. (I still can't believe you sang the entire Texas state song on our third date.) Because of you, I am my truest, best self, and the sweet respite between us is God's most precious grace. My lover and friend, I always want you to have the best I have to give. I'd be lost without you; oh how I love you, and thank you. What a beautiful life we're building.

ABOUT THE AUTHOR

Ashley Abercrombie fought to overcome addiction, rape, abortion, perfectionism, and dysfunctional relationships to become an honest, whole, and free woman (most days). She wore a mask more than half her life, and considers herself too old and too annoyed to ever put that thing on again. She has been leading in urban, multicultural, racially diverse ministry for more than fifteen years. She has an unrelenting passion for justice, particularly anti–human trafficking and mass incarceration initiatives. Ashley is an executive board member of Treasures, her favorite nonprofit, which reaches and supports women in the sex industry and victims of sexual exploitation while training leaders globally. She is an advocate, speaker, and writer featured in many magazines and digital outlets. Ashley and her husband, Cody, are almost brain-dead from sleep deprivation because of raising their two incredible sons, Levi and Lucas, in their beautiful neighborhood in New York City.

Connect with
ASHLEY

ASHABERCROMBIE.ORG

Don't miss her podcast, *Why Tho?*,
with Tiffany Bluhm and Ashley Abercrombie,
available wherever you find your podcasts.

ashabercrombie ashleyabercrombienyc

ashabercrombie

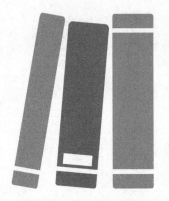

LIKE THIS BOOK?

Consider sharing it with others!

- Share or mention the book on your social media platforms. Use the hashtag **#RiseoftheTruthTeller**.

- Write a book review on your blog or on a retailer site.

- Pick up a copy for friends, family, or anyone who you think would enjoy and be challenged by its message!

- Share this message on Twitter, Facebook, or Instagram: **I loved #RiseoftheTruthTeller by @AshAbercrombie @ReadBakerBooks**

- Recommend this book for your church, workplace, book club, or class.

- Follow Baker Books on social media and tell us what you like.

f **ReadBakerBooks**

🐦 **ReadBakerBooks**

ReadBakerBooks